The 21 Most Dangerous Questions of the Bible

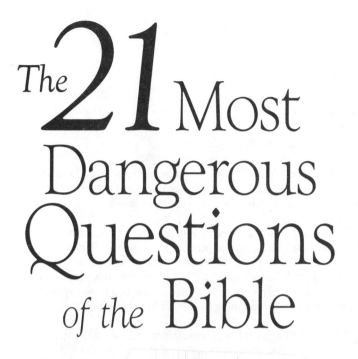

Dave
Earley

BARBOUR
PUBLISHING

Published by Barbour Publishing, Inc., P.O. Box 719, Uhrichsville, Ohio 44683, www.barbourbooks.com

Our mission is to publish and distribute inspirational products offering exceptional value and biblical encouragement to the masses.

ecpa Member of the
Evangelical Christian
Publishers Association

Printed in the United States of America.

Acknowledgments

Teamwork is the fuel that allows common people to attain uncommon results. If this book attains extraordinary results it will be because of the efforts of a capable and qualified team.

- Cathy, you are my very best friend. Thank you for being such an encouragement, and for praying over, editing, critiquing, and proofing every word.

- Carol, for your consistent encouragement.

- Sandy, for modeling grace under fire.

- Steve, for being my favorite brother.

- Dave Wheeler, Rebecca Autry, Neil Grobler, David Brinkley, Chip Stallings, Becky Mahle, and Julie Moore— you are wonderful LCMT teammates.

- Elmer Towns—you set the pace.

- The Barbour team, for asking me to write this book.

- Paul Muckley, you are a joy to work with.

- Les Stobbe, for opening the door.

- Kelly Williams and Annie Tipton, for managing the in-house processes, and Sharon Dean, for handling the typesetting.

Contents

Introduction

We had known each other a year and a half. Cathy had just spent a summer in Virginia working and teaching Sunday school. I had spent the summer in New York City doing evangelism and discipleship. For months, I had fasted one day a week, praying about whether or not she was the girl I should marry. I was 99 percent sure.

When I returned from New York, Cathy fixed me a great spaghetti dinner. She looked gorgeous as the joy of the Lord shone through her face. During dinner a dangerous question kept running through my head. Before I knew what had happened, I blurted out, "I need to ask you something."

"What?" she smiled.

"Would you. . ."

"Yes?" she asked.

". . .um. . .pass me the salt?" I said with a sigh.

After dinner we sat on the couch talking. I made the mistake of looking into her sparkling green eyes. Everything got misty. It was as if time stopped—or at least shifted into slow motion. My head swam, and I heard an indistinguishable tune floating through my mind. The dangerous question kept popping into my brain. My heart pounded.

I couldn't take it for another second. I had to ask the question. Suddenly, I grabbed her shoulders.

"I need to ask you a question." I swallowed.

"What?" she smiled, confused by my sudden seriousness.

"Would you. . ."

"Yes?" she responded, now frowning at me like I was an idiot.

I took a deep breath. "Cathy," I said with great gravity. "Will you. . ." I gulped. The words were literally choking me.

"Yes?" she said, a smile slowly forming on her lips. She leaned closer, now aware of what I was about to ask.

"Will you. . ." I gulped again. ". . .marry me?"

More Dangerous Questions

The book you hold in your hands is a simple study of what I consider the twenty-one riskiest questions in the Bible. It considers nearly two dozen questions that created defining moments in the lives of significant Bible figures. These timeless questions can be life changing for you, too, as you ask them of yourself and wrestle to a response.

When you first saw the title *The 21 Most Dangerous Questions of the Bible*, you may have asked yourself, "Dangerous for whom or for what?" That depends on how you answer these twenty-one questions. Respond one way, and you'll create grave hazards for the status quo—and the kingdom of darkness. Answer in the opposite, and you'll bring about peril for yourself and the world around you.

We also thought of calling this book *The 21 Most Important Questions* or *The 21 Most Defining Questions* or *The 21 Major Watershed Questions* or *The 21 Tipping Point Questions of the Bible*. Each question covered is that significant and potentially powerful.

Let me say that if you are thoroughly content with your life as it is and the direction the world is heading, *don't* read this book and consider these questions. If you are happy to have an unexamined faith, this probably is not the book for you. But if you long for change and yearn to make a difference—if you are willing to risk everything with the hope of coming out better on the other side—then, please, read on.

This is an unsafe book. I hope at times to make you a little uncomfortable. My intent is not so much to *inform* as to *transform*.

These questions will force you to evaluate what you really believe about God and His Word. They will challenge the level of your faith and commitment. Hopefully, they will change your life for the better.

What Is Man That You Are Mindful of Him?

PSALM 8:4

It's always one of the highlights of my day. At ten o'clock each evening, I pull on a jacket and get the dog's leash from the closet. Then Rocky, our miniature schnauzer, and I walk out into the night.

Most evenings, when the sky is clear, I can't keep myself from looking up. I can't help gawking at the incredible display in the heavens. We live in the country where there is less ambient light, so the stars, moon, and planets are gloriously apparent in the heavens. The sight is truly breathtaking. By the time I return home, I usually have a kink in my neck from stargazing.

Recently, for my birthday, Cathy got me a telescope. Now, on warm nights, I can gaze to my heart's content at the silver diamond stars gleaming on their black velvet background.

Of course, I'm not the first person to be mesmerized by the stars. Three thousand years ago, a young shepherd was also awestruck by the nightly display that quietly occurs in the heavens. What David saw and how it made him feel ended up as a song. I don't know if you've sung it before, but I'll bet you've read it. Embedded in that song is a potentially dangerous question.

O LORD, our Lord, how majestic is your name in all the earth! You have set your glory above the heavens. From the lips of children and infants you have ordained praise because of your enemies, to silence the foe and the avenger.

*When I consider your heavens, the work of your fingers, the moon and the stars, which you have set in place, **what is man that you are mindful of him,** the son of man that you care for him?*

You made him a little lower than the heavenly beings and crowned him with glory and honor. You made him ruler over the works of your hands; you put everything under his feet: all flocks and herds, and the beasts of the field, the birds of the air, and the fish of the sea, all that swim the paths of the seas.

PSALM 8:1–8

As he gazed into the sky, David was enthralled by the vast glory of the heavens—the heavens that the Lord God made and owns. Deep within David's heart, a question arose: "What is man that you are mindful of him, the son of man that you care for him?" (Psalm 8:4). David was awed by the amazing heavens, yet he was more astounded that the Lord, who can make such immense works of art, would have any interest in the human race. His question and its answer led him to a profound sense of significance.

The Heavens Are Amazing

When I look at the stars, I'm floored to remember that they are so incredibly far away that the distance has to be measured in light-*years*. The speed of light is almost beyond comprehension—186,000 miles per second. Therefore a light-year equals 5.87 *trillion* miles!

The distance around the earth is about twenty-five thousand miles. So a "particle" of light traveling at the speed of light can zip around the earth about seven or eight times in just one second. Yet our own galaxy is so vast that we measure the distance to stars within the Milky Way in light-years—the distance light travels in a year.

I am also impressed with the incredible *number* of stars visible on a clear night. Consider that the total number of individual stars visible to the naked eye in both the northern and the southern celestial hemispheres is about six thousand. Therefore, if I took the time to count, I could see at most about three thousand stars at the same time. Yet our Milky Way galaxy has been found to contain two hundred thousand *million* stars! If somebody could count three stars per second, after one hundred years he would have counted less than five percent of this number.

Scientists now estimate that the total number of stars in the observable universe is 10^{25} (1 followed by 25 zeros). Using an extremely fast computer, making ten thousand million calculations per second, it would still require thirty million years of nonstop counting to number those stars![1]

Wow!

Yet God knows each star by name:

He determines the number of the stars and calls them each by name.

PSALM 147:4

No wonder stargazing brought David to worship, saying, "O Lord, our Lord, how majestic is your name in all the earth! You have set your glory above the heavens" (Psalm 8:1). No wonder David was compelled to ask, "What is man that you are mindful of him, the son of man that you care for him?" (Psalm 8:4).

What Is Man?

David asked, "What is man?" If we allow science to answer this
dangerous question, we're told that man (and woman) is an
animal, the highest form of life, a bipedal primate belonging to
the mammalian species, *Homo sapiens,* the product of millions
of years of evolution, a tiny creature in an immense universe.
Such sterile answers, coupled with the massive vastness of the
universe, can bring people to the dangerous brink of despair,
drowning in their own insignificance.

Yet when David asked the question some three thousand
years ago, he was swept away by awe. He responded in
worship, sharing a prayer, writing a hymn, and uttering
a strong statement of praise. Instead of feeling lost as a
meaningless speck in an immeasurable universe, David was
thrilled to realize that the same Lord who made the heavens
made him. The same God, who knows countless stars by name,
knew *his* name!

David discovered that the same God who is big enough to
create gigantic galaxies is small enough to be vitally involved
in the day-to-day dealings of individual people. The innate
dignity of humanity lies not in who *we* are, but rather in who
God is. The issue is not who do *I* say I am, but instead, who
does *God* say I am?

In an article on the Internet Infidels Web site titled
"Death and the Meaning of Life," Keith Augustine makes a
game attempt to argue that atheists can find meaning in life.
Yet when he answers the question, "What is man?" he comes
up empty. The writer states that death is inevitable and leads
to "a dreamless sleep from which we will never awake, our
consciousness snuffed out forever." He continues by saying,
"As far as science can tell, there is no greater purpose for
our lives." Yet he also argues that life can be meaningful.[2]
To which I say, "You've got to be kidding!"

David, on the other hand, was able to ask a dangerous question and come through with a meaningful answer. Instead of saying, "There is no God," David saw everything through the lens of God. When he asked, "What is man that you are mindful of him?" his God-centered understanding of the universe led him to a strong sense of personal identity, a marvelous dignity, a deep significance, and a God-given purpose. Reread his grateful words of praise:

> *You made him a little lower than the heavenly beings and crowned him with glory and honor. You made him ruler over the works of your hands; you put everything under his feet: all flocks and herds, and the beasts of the field, the birds of the air, and the fish of the sea, all that swim the paths of the seas.*
>
> PSALM 8:5–8

Look at those words more closely. "You made him a little lower than the heavenly beings and crowned him with glory and honor." Humanity has dignity because we are *not* the product of chance; we are the masterwork of the sovereign Creator.

God made us. Not only that, He dignified us by placing us "a little lower than the heavenly beings," crowning us with glory. And beyond that, He elevated us to the position of "ruler" over the works of His hands. He put *everything* under our feet, including "all flocks and herds, and the beasts of the field, the birds of the air, and the fish of the sea, all that swim the paths of the seas."

David may have only been a poor shepherd, but his clear understanding of his identity as a creation of God gave him the confidence to face a giant. Because David recognized that the God who made the heavens also knew his name, he was able to lead armies to victory and wear the crown of a king.

Who Are You?

According to Psalm 8, you are much more than an animal or the random product of millions of years of evolution. You are the unique handiwork of the most intelligent and powerful being imaginable. God, the creator and sustainer of the vast heavens, made you and gave you an important status on this planet. You were given dominion and dignity, position and privilege.

There is no reason to feel insignificant or that life is without meaning. You were made on purpose, with purpose. Your life matters. You can make a difference. What happens to you is important. Someone is watching, and He does care.

Notes

1. Distances and measurements were primarily taken from the article "Counting the Stars: *The Vastness of the Universe Is Cause for Joy, not Loneliness,*" by Werner Gitt, Answers in Genesis, http://www. answersingenesis.org/creation/v19/i2/stars.asp (accessed June 18, 2007).
2. Keith Augustine, "Death and the Meaning of Life," The Secular Web, http://www.infidels.org/library/modern/features/2000/augustine1. html#F2 (accessed June 18, 2007).

Who Do You Say I Am?

MATTHEW 16:15

Who is Jesus?

Is He a great teacher, a good man, a gifted prophet—or something more? Is He legend, liar, lunatic—or someone else? These are dangerous questions. How we answer them has important ramifications because the identity of Jesus Christ is the foundation of Christianity. As John Stott has noted,

> *Essentially Christianity is Christ. The person and work of Christ are the rock upon which the Christian religion is built. If he is not who he said he was and did not do what he said he came to do, the foundation is undermined and the whole superstructure will collapse. Take Christ from Christianity, and you disembowel it; there is practically nothing left. Christ is the [center] of Christianity; all else is circumference.*[1]

Even more importantly, the identity of Jesus Christ is the basis of the salvation of a soul from sin and its punishment. Belief in Jesus is the only way to experience eternal life.

> *"Salvation is found in no one else, for there is no other name under heaven given to men by which we must be saved."*
>
> ACTS 4:12

"Whoever believes in the Son has eternal life, but whoever rejects the Son will not see life, for God's wrath remains on him."

JOHN 3:36

"Who Do You Say I Am?"

Peter and the other disciples had been following Jesus for over three years. They had seen Him do things no other man had ever done and heard Him say things no one had ever said. Jesus knew that His time on earth was drawing to a close. He wanted Peter and the others to have one fact firmly fixed in their minds—His identity. In order to withstand all that lay ahead, they would need to understand exactly who Jesus really was. In order to clarify their convictions, Jesus asked them a dangerous question.

> *When Jesus came to the region of Caesarea Philippi, he asked his disciples, "Who do people say the Son of Man is?"*
>
> *They replied, "Some say John the Baptist; others say Elijah; and still others, Jeremiah or one of the prophets."*
>
> *"But what about you?" he asked. **"Who do you say I am?"***

MATTHEW 16:13–15

The answer to Jesus' question had been forming in Peter's mind and heart for several years. Hearing all he had heard and seeing all he had seen had solidified his convictions. Confidently, he gave a succinct answer, voicing one of the most significant statements ever made.

Simon Peter answered, "You are the Christ, the Son of the living God."

Jesus replied, "Blessed are you, Simon son of Jonah, for this was not revealed to you by man, but by my Father in heaven."

MATTHEW 16:16–17

"You Are the Christ"

When Peter announced that Jesus was "the Christ," he was speaking of the long-awaited Anointed One. "The Christ," or "Messiah," was the One set apart by the Father and anointed with the Holy Spirit to be the Chief Priest of His people (see Deuteronomy 18:15–18; Isaiah 55:4; Luke 24:19; Acts 3:22, 7:37).

Peter and the others had seen how Jesus uniquely fulfilled the prophecies about the Messiah. His birth, life, death, and resurrection were described in amazing detail hundreds and, in some instances thousands, of years prior to their occurrence.

The name of His great-great-great grandfather was predicted. The place of His birth was predicted. So was the visit by the wise men, the gifts the wise men brought, the appearance of the Christmas star, and Herod's attempt to kill Him. Jesus' trip to Egypt to avoid Herod was predicted. Those are merely a few of the fulfilled prophecies about Jesus' birth.

In observing the unique and astounding reality of the impressive prophecies fulfilled by the birth and life of Jesus, my friend and internationally recognized Bible scholar, H. L. Wilmington, poses the question:

Can any other founder of a known religion point to a similar written record of his life already in existence hundreds of years before his birth? . . . The answer is no.[2]

In the Old Testament, there are as many as 332 distinct predictions which are literally fulfilled in Christ.[3] Astronomer and mathematician Peter Stoner, in his book *Science Speaks*, offers an analysis showing that it is impossible for the precise statements about the Messiah to be fulfilled in a single person by mere coincidence. He estimates that the chance of only *eight* of these prophecies being fulfilled in the life of one man is only 1 in 10 to the 17th power.[4] That is the number one followed by seventeen zeroes, or one chance in 100,000,000,000,000,000! (Compare this to winning the lottery, with odds of "one in a million" as one followed by only six zeroes.)

In order to understand how amazing it is that one man fulfilled just eight of the prophecies Jesus fulfilled, consider this example:

> *Take 100,000,000,000,000,000 silver dollars and lay them on the face of Texas [with its approximate land area of 262,000 square miles]. They will cover all of the state two feet deep. Now mark one of these silver dollars and stir the whole mass thoroughly, all over the state. Blindfold a man and tell him that he can travel as far as he wishes, but he must pick up one silver dollar and say that this is the right one.*
>
> *What chance would he have of getting the right one? Just the same chance that the prophets would have had of writing these eight prophecies and having them all come true in any one man.[5]*

That is one man fulfilling only *eight* of the prophecies regarding the Messiah. Yet Jesus fulfilled 332!

Say it with me, "Wow!" Jesus fulfilled the prophecies as only the Messiah could.

"The Son of the Living God"

Peter also called Jesus "the son of the living God." The title "the living God" was a name reserved for Jehovah Himself (see Deuteronomy 5:26; Joshua 3:10; 1 Samuel 17:26, 36; 2 Kings 19:4, 16; Psalm 42:2, 84:2; Daniel 6:26; Hosea 1:10). For Peter to call Jesus by this name was to clearly state his belief that Jesus was no mere man—He was God. Why would Peter believe that?

1. Jesus did things only God can do.
Jesus walked on a stormy sea (Matthew 14:25). He rebuked the wind and it obeyed Him (Luke 8:24; note that He did not ask God to calm the sea; He accomplished that by Himself). Jesus turned water into wine (John 2:6–11) and cured a centurion's servant without any contact with the ill man (Matthew 8:5–13). He fed massive crowds with as little as a boy's lunch (Matthew 14:15–21, 15:34–38). At the pool of Bethesda in Jerusalem, Jesus healed a man who had been unable to walk for thirty-eight years (John 5:1–9). He cast out demons (Matthew 17:14–20, 15:22–28; Mark 1:23–28, 5:1–19), healed the sick (Matthew 8:14–16, 9:20–22; Mark 7:32–37), cured the leprous (Matthew 8:2–4; Luke 17:11–19), mended the lame (Matthew 9:2–8), and gave sight to the blind (Matthew 12:22; Mark 8:22–26). Jesus even raised the dead (Matthew 9:18–26; Luke 7:12–16; John 11:1–46)!

2. Jesus accepted worship.
Even though He clearly knew that only God was to be worshipped, Jesus accepted worship on several occasions. He did not refuse the worship offered by a leper (Matthew 8:2–3), his own disciples (Matthew 14:33), a Canaanite woman (Matthew 15:25), and a man born blind (John 9:38).

3. *Jesus displayed characteristics or attributes that can only be true of God.*

Jesus not only had power over disease, death, demons, wind, and waves, He also displayed omniscience in that He knew people's lives, even their secret histories (John 4:16–19). He knew the inner thoughts of people, knew all people, and what was in people (Mark 2:8; Luke 5:22; John 2:24–25). He essentially knew everything (John 16:30).

4. *Jesus made claims that only God can make.*

When He claimed to have the authority to forgive sins, He backed it up by healing a lame man (Mark 2:1–12).

> *"Why are you thinking these things? Which is easier: to say to the paralytic, 'Your sins are forgiven,' or to say, 'Get up, take your mat and walk'? But that you may know that the Son of Man has authority on earth to forgive sins. . . ." He said to the paralytic, "I tell you, get up, take your mat and go home." He got up, took his mat and walked out in full view of them all.*
>
> MARK 2:8–12

Jesus claimed to be able to give life (John 5:21) and to be the source of life (John 14:6). He further claimed to have the divine authority and responsibility for eternal judgment.

> *"Moreover, the Father judges no one, but has entrusted all judgment to the Son. . . . I tell you the truth, a time is coming and has now come when the dead will hear the voice of the Son of God and those who hear will live. For as the Father has life in himself, so he has granted the Son to have life in himself. And he has given him authority to judge because he is the Son of Man. Do not be amazed at this, for a time is coming when all who are in their graves*

will hear his voice and come out—those who have done
good will rise to live, and those who have done evil will
rise to be condemned."

JOHN 5:22, 25–29

5. *Jesus equated a response to Him with a response to God.*

He said that to know Him was to know God (John 8:19,
14:7); to believe in Him was to believe in God (John 12:44);
to see Him was to see God (John 12:45, 14:9); to hate Him
was to hate God (John 15:23); and to honor Him was to
honor God (John 5:22–23).

Jesus' claims of divinity were so obvious that the Jews
wanted to stone Him for blasphemy.

"I and the Father are one."
   Again the Jews picked up stones to stone him, but Jesus
said to them, "I have shown you many great miracles from
the Father. For which of these do you stone me?"
   "We are not stoning you for any of these," replied the
Jews, "but for blasphemy, because you, a mere man, claim
to be God."

JOHN 10:30–33

Jesus said to them, "My Father is always at his work to
this very day, and I, too, am working." For this reason
the Jews tried all the harder to kill him; not only was he
breaking the Sabbath, but he was even calling God his
own Father, making himself equal with God.

JOHN 5:17–18

His bold claims reached the pinnacle when he claimed to
be Jehovah, the great "I AM" described in Exodus 3:13–14.

"I tell you the truth," Jesus answered, "before Abraham was born, I am!" At this, they picked up stones to stone him.

JOHN 8:58–59

Who Is Jesus?

Jesus claimed to be God. You and I are faced with a question: Who is Jesus, really?

In his famous book, *Mere Christianity*, Oxford professor and former skeptic C. S. Lewis made this statement:

> *A man who was merely a man and said the sort of things Jesus said would not be a great moral teacher. He would either be a lunatic—on the level with a man who says he is a poached egg—or he would be the devil of hell. You must take your choice. Either this was, and is, the Son of God, or else a madman or something worse. You can shut him up for a fool or you can fall at his feet and call him Lord and God. But let us not come with any patronizing nonsense about his being a great human teacher. He has not left that open to us.*[6]

After studying the facts for himself, Lewis concluded that Jesus was indeed God. He spent the rest of his life using his gift for writing to tell the world about Jesus.

Who is Jesus? Peter believed that Jesus is Lord and God. He became the leading spokesman for the Christian faith and died as a martyr for that faith.

So let me ask you: Who is Jesus?

Do you believe that He is God?

Will you put Him above everything else in your life?

Will you make Him the focal point of your day?

Will you make Him central in your decisions about the future?

Will the rest of your life reveal your faith in Him?

Notes

1. John R. W. Stott, *Basic Christianity* (Downers Grove, IL: Intervarsity Press, 1958), 21.
2. H. L. Wilmington, quote taken from a lecture given by Dr. Wilmington at Liberty Bible Institute, Lynchburg, VA, on Oct. 21, 1982.
3. Floyd Hamilton, *The Basis of Christian Faith* (New York: Harper and Row, 1964), 160.
4. Peter Stoner, *Science Speaks* (Chicago: Moody Press, 1963), 100.
5. Ibid, 107.
6. C. S. Lewis, *Mere Christianity* (New York: The MacMillan Company, 1952), 41.

3

Do You Love Me?

JOHN 21:15–17

Serving Jesus is often not easy. Each month, as many as two thousand pastors and their families leave the ministry never to return.[1] Only God knows how many good church members drop out of ministry each year and stop serving in their churches.

The apostle Peter knew the desire to quit. One minute he had boasted that he would follow Jesus to prison or even death (Luke 22:33). The next thing he knew, he had denied Jesus three times (Luke 22:54–62). He wanted to quit, run away, and hide. Discouraged, Peter and several of the disciples went back to what they did before they were called—fishing.

Yet God is a God of the second chance. Jesus, the resurrected Christ, surprised His disciples as they were fishing on the Sea of Galilee. In their encounter, Jesus asked Peter one of the most significant and penetrating—in fact, one of the most dangerous—questions ever asked.

Do You Love Me?

> *When they had finished eating, Jesus said to Simon Peter,*
> *"Simon son of John, do you truly love me more than*
> *these?"*
> *"Yes, Lord," he said, "you know that I love you."*
> *Jesus said, "Feed my lambs."*

> *Again Jesus said, "Simon son of John, do you truly love me?"*
>
> *He answered, "Yes, Lord, you know that I love you."*
>
> *Jesus said, "Take care of my sheep."*
>
> *The third time he said to him, "Simon son of John, do you love me?"*
>
> *Peter was hurt because Jesus asked him the third time,* **"Do you love me?"** *He said, "Lord, you know all things; you know that I love you."*
>
> *Jesus said, "Feed my sheep."*
>
> JOHN 21:15–17

Three times Jesus asked Peter, "Do you love me?"

Three times Peter answered, "You know that I love you."

Three times Jesus responded by giving Peter a responsibility: "Feed my lambs; shepherd my sheep; feed my sheep."

This scenario, summarized by John in three little verses, shows us that the essence of effective ministry will always be an overflow of our love relationship with Jesus. If Peter hoped to accomplish anything good in the future, it would only be because of His love for Jesus.

Initially, this pointed question hurt Peter. But his life was wonderfully changed as a result of Jesus' query. Oswald Chambers writes:

> *The Lord's questions always reveal the true me to myself. . . . Rarely, but probably once in each of our lives, He will back us into a corner where He will hurt us with His piercing questions. Then we will realize that we do love Him far more deeply than our words can ever say.*[2]

Do You Love Me?

Jesus might have asked Peter all kinds of questions that day. If I had been in Jesus' position, I might have asked, "Why did you deny me?" or "What were you thinking?" or "What do you have to say for yourself?" But that's not the angle Jesus took. He asked, "Do you love me?"

I don't think the question implies that Peter lacked love for Jesus. Instead, the Lord penetrated to the core of what a life of dynamic discipleship is all about. As Jesus taught, the greatest command is, "Love the Lord your God with all your heart and with all your soul and with all your mind" (Matthew 22:37). Christianity is a relationship, not a religion.

Note also that Jesus did not ask Peter if he was a gifted speaker, a talented leader, or even a person of sound character. Jesus didn't inquire about Peter's seminary training or Bible knowledge. Those things are important, but they're not *the* issue. *The* issue is quite simple. The one basic qualification for lasting ministry is found in Jesus' question, "Do you love me?" Love for Jesus is the only motive for ministry that will endure the test.

I find it interesting that Jesus didn't even ask Peter, "Do you love *people*?" Loving people is important for ministering. But loving Jesus is more important. Pastor Richard Tow writes:

> *Ministry does not begin with a love for people. It begins with a love for God and that love overflows to people. If we minister only out of a humanistic love for people we will be people-pleasers rather than God-pleasers. We ultimately will not help them nor serve the purposes of God. But if everything begins with a holy love toward the Lord we will love people and we will serve their best interest—not always their whims and desires but always*

their best interest. Nothing will keep ministry on course
like a deep love for the Lord. Nothing will carry us
through the hard times like a sincere devotion to Christ.[3]

Nothing Is More Important Than Our Relationship with Jesus

Three times Jesus asked Peter, "Do you love me?" Notice that He asked this question *before* giving Peter the commission to shepherd His sheep. Why?

Jesus wanted Peter (and us, for that matter) never to forget that the chief criteria of enduring, effective ministry is loving Him above all else. Love of Christ is central; all else is peripheral.

Too often we assume that the prime prerequisite for serving Jesus well is great giftedness, immense talent, or impressive academic credentials. But Peter and most of the other disciples were ordinary fisherman from a backward part of the country. They were nobodies until Jesus called them.

The main requirement for making a difference *for* Jesus is being in love *with* Jesus. Jesus repeated the question three times because He wanted the concept to be crystal clear: Nothing is more important than our relationship with Jesus.

A Most Dangerous Disciple

When Peter realized the gravity of Jesus' question, and when he was able to respond positively, his life changed significantly. He became a most dangerous disciple. Just a few weeks later, the former coward, a denier of Jesus, stood before thousands of people, boldly preaching Christ. Amazingly, three thousand people gave their lives to the Lord and the Christian church was born (Acts 2:1–41). Beyond that, Peter was used of God to open the door of salvation to non-Jews (Acts 10:34–48).

What made Peter so positively dangerous? He discovered His passion for Jesus and continued to build the relationship. Before he and the other disciples launched their ministry, they held an intense prayer meeting (Acts 1:12–14). He was careful to maintain a regular hour of prayer (Acts 3:1). He, along with the other disciples, made a conscious decision to give their attention to prayer and the ministry of the Word (Acts 6:4).

Real Ministry for Jesus Flows Out of Our Relationship with Jesus

What we do *for* God is only a reflection of the relationship we have *with* God. If we want to be able to do great things, we need to have a great relationship. If we want to have a ministry that is strong, our relationship must be strong.

Oswald Chambers was a man others recognized as being abandoned to God. He was a Scottish itinerant preacher and Bible college founder. In his early forties he died of a ruptured appendix far from home in Egypt while ministering to British troops during World War I. His meditations on the Christian life, collected in the daily devotional classic *My Utmost for His Highest*, have enriched millions. Chambers deeply understood the essential nature of our relationship with Jesus.

> *The main thing about Christianity is not the work we do, but the relationship we maintain, and the atmosphere produced by that relationship. That is all God asks us to look after, and it is the one thing that is being continually assailed.*[4]

The Love-Slave

Samuel Logan Brengle was a Salvation Army preacher. While street preaching in a very rough section of Boston, he was severely injured when a drunk threw a brick at him. His writings are powerfully pungent with the aroma of a man who knew that real ministry flowed from a red-hot relationship with Jesus.

Using the imagery of the apostle Paul, Brengle viewed his relationship with Jesus as that of voluntary servitude fueled by love.

> *The love-slave is altogether at his Master's service. He is all eyes for his master. He watches. He is all ears for his master. He listens. His mind is willing. His hands are ready. His feet are swift. To sit at the master's feet and look into his loved face; to listen to his voice and catch his words; to run on his errands; to do his bidding; to share his privations and sorrows; to watch at his door; to guard his honor; to praise his name; to defend his person; to seek and promote his interests, and, if needs be, to die for his dear sake, this is the joy of the slave of love, and this he counts his perfect freedom.*[5]

The Disciple Jesus Loved

As Jesus asked Peter the probing question, "Do you love me?", the young apostle John eavesdropped. He watched, he listened, and he learned. Later, he wrote of the event in his Gospel. But he also wrote it into his life.

John lived an amazing life of enduring, effective ministry. He was co-pastor of the thriving church of Jerusalem. He wrote one of the four Gospel accounts of Jesus' life as well as three epistles, and he was privileged to be given the Revelation that concludes our Bible. In spite of persistent heartache and persecution, he kept going strong up through his nineties. What was his secret? Rather than identifying himself as "John, the pastor of First Church in Jerusalem," or "John, the author of the Revelation," or "John, the apostle," he only identified himself as "the disciple whom Jesus loved."

> *Now there was leaning on Jesus' bosom one of his disciples, whom Jesus loved.*
>
> JOHN 13:23 KJV

> *When Jesus saw his mother there, and the disciple whom he loved standing nearby, he said to his mother, "Dear woman, here is your son."*
>
> JOHN 19:26

> *So she* [Mary Magdalene] *came running to Simon Peter and the other disciple, the one Jesus loved, and said, "They have taken the Lord out of the tomb, and we don't know where they have put him!"*
>
> JOHN 20:2

> *Peter turned and saw that the disciple whom Jesus loved was following them.*
>
> JOHN 21:20

Obviously Jesus loved all the disciples, but John was the most aware and appreciative. John lived by this principle: First we receive God's love for us, then out will flow our love for God and others.

Notes

1. Global Pastors Network newsletter, August 3, 2004.
2. Oswald Chambers, *My Utmost for His Highest, Updated Edition* (Grand Rapids, MI: Discovery House Publishers, 1992), March 2 entry.
3. Richard Tow, "Ministry Essentials: Fortifying the Foundation #47," http://www.sermoncentral.com/sermon.asp?SermonID=83277& ContributorID=10438 (accessed June 19, 2007).
4. Oswald Chambers, *My Utmost for His Highest* (Uhrichsville, OH: Barbour Publishing, Inc., 1999) August 4 entry.
5. Samuel Logan Brengle, *Love-Slaves* (London: Salvationist Publishing and Supplies, Ltd., 1929), http://wesley.nnu.edu/wesleyctr/ books/0001-0100/HDM0021.PDF accessed February 12, 2007, p. 4.

Jesus I Know, and I Know About Paul, but Who Are You?

ACTS 19:15

Reality television shows find a limitless supply of people who will eat insects, lie in a bathtub of snakes, or humiliate themselves trying to sing, dance, or answer trivia questions. Why? They want to be noticed. They want, like the characters in the 1980 movie *Fame,* for you to "remember my name."

A desire for fame and influence is nothing new. Paul encountered the same passion for popularity and power nearly two thousand years ago in Ephesus.

> *While Apollos was at Corinth, Paul took the road through the interior and arrived at Ephesus. . . . Some Jews who went around driving out evil spirits tried to invoke the name of the Lord Jesus over those who were demon-possessed. They would say, "In the name of Jesus, whom Paul preaches, I command you to come out."*
>
> ACTS 19:1, 13

These men who were casting out demons in the name of Jesus did not *know* Jesus. They had only *heard* of Him—and they soon discovered that a secondhand relationship with Jesus is not sufficient when encountering the dark spirits of the devil. Merely saying the words, "In the name of Jesus, whom Paul preaches, I command you to come out," was not enough.

> *Seven sons of Sceva, a Jewish chief priest, were doing this.*
> *One day the evil spirit answered them,* ***"Jesus I know,***
> ***and I know about Paul, but who are you?"*** *Then*
> *the man who had the evil spirit jumped on them and*
> *overpowered them all. He gave them such a beating that*
> *they ran out of the house naked and bleeding.*
>
> ACTS 19:14–16

Ouch! Dealing with the devil is not fun and games. It is serious business that requires a mature relationship with Jesus Christ. It also demands that we ask ourselves a very dangerous question.

Look again at Acts 19:15. Before provoking the severe beating of the sons of Sceva, one of the evil spirits asked a profound question.

> *"Jesus I know, and I know about Paul, but who are you?"*
>
> ACTS 19:15

"Jesus I Know"

One of the evil spirits declared, "Jesus I know!" The name of Jesus was, and is, certainly well known in hell.

The name of Jesus was well known to Satan. It was Jesus who Satan tried to have killed as an infant in Bethlehem (Matthew 2:13–18). It was Jesus who Satan personally tried to tempt in the wilderness (Luke 4:1–13). It was Jesus who the devil tried to have thrown over a cliff at the beginning of His ministry (Luke 4:28–30). Of course, it was Jesus who Satan prompted Judas to betray to be crucified (John 13:27–30; 18:1ff).

The identity of Jesus was also well known to demons.

Whenever the evil spirits saw him, they fell down before him and cried out, "You are the Son of God."

MARK 3:11

Moreover, demons came out of many people, shouting, "You are the Son of God!" But he rebuked them and would not allow them to speak, because they knew he was the Christ.

LUKE 4:41

Demons were cast out in the name of Jesus.

Finally Paul became so troubled that he turned around and said to the spirit, "In the name of Jesus Christ I command you to come out of her!" At that moment the spirit left her.

ACTS 16:18

"Paul I Know"

The name of Paul was also well known in hell. Before the evil spirits prompted the possessed man to beat the sons of Sceva, one of them declared, "I know about Paul."

When Paul, the leading persecutor of the church, switched sides and converted to Christ, the news was received coldly in hell (Acts 8:1–3, 9:1–22). Hell certainly noted with anger that Paul's preaching to the Gentiles was so powerful he was accused of turning the world upside down (Acts 17:6 KJV)! While in Ephesus, prior to the beating of the sons of Sceva, Paul had developed quite a ministry and reputation. Others wanted the power he had.

> *God did extraordinary miracles through Paul, so that*
> *even handkerchiefs and aprons that had touched him were*
> *taken to the sick, and their illnesses were cured and the*
> *evil spirits left them. Some Jews who went around driving*
> *out evil spirits tried to invoke the name of the Lord Jesus*
> *over those who were demon-possessed. They would say, "In*
> *the name of Jesus, whom Paul preaches, I command you to*
> *come out."*
>
> Acts 19:11–13

Merely mouthing words didn't work—just ask the
sons of Sceva. There needed to be a dangerous life support-
ing those words—a life like Paul's, that was dangerous
to hell.

In his classic book *Why Revival Tarries*, Leonard Ravenhill
explained why Paul was well known in hell. Building on
the theme of Paul viewing himself as crucified with Christ,
Ravenhill writes,

> *He had no ambitions—and so had nothing to be jealous*
> *about. He had no reputation—and so had nothing to*
> *fight about. He had no possessions—and therefore nothing*
> *to worry about. He had no "rights"—so therefore he could*
> *not suffer wrong. He was already broken—so no one could*
> *break him. He was "dead"—so none could kill him. He*
> *was less than the least of the least—so who could humble*
> *him? He had suffered the loss of all things—so who could*
> *defraud him? Does this throw any light on why the demon*
> *said, "Paul I know"? Over this God-intoxicated man, hell*
> *suffered headaches.*[1]

"Who Are You?"

Our discussion circles back to the main issue. The demons asked the sons of Sceva one of the most dangerous questions that can be asked:

> *"Jesus I know, and I know about Paul, but who are you?"*

"Who are you?" In other words, "We've never heard of you. Your faces don't hang on the walls of hell's post office. There's no 'Wanted' poster saying APPROACH CAREFULLY— CONSIDERED ARMED AND VERY DANGEROUS."

Clearly, the sons of Sceva had no answer to the demons' question. As we have read, the lone man possessed by the demons beat up Sceva's boys and sent them running for their lives (Acts 19:14–16).

Does the Devil Know Your Name?

I don't claim the amazing authority of the Lord Jesus Christ or the apostle Paul. But I believe I can live a positively dangerous life. I hope to live so completely for God's kingdom that I am known by those in the kingdom of darkness. I want to give hell a headache.

What about you? If an evil spirit questioned your identity, what would you say? How would you answer? Are you becoming a dangerous Christian? Are you famous in hell? Do demons shudder at the mention of your name?

How would you respond if a demon asked you the same question? "Jesus I know, and I know about Paul, *but who are you?*"

Prayer Is the Battle

> *For our struggle is not against flesh and blood, but against*
> *the rulers, against the authorities, against the powers of*
> *this dark world and against the spiritual forces of evil*
> *in the heavenly realms.*
>
> EPHESIANS 6:12

We are seeing an increased level of satanic activity in North America. We hear more and more accounts of church members and churches bound by demonic oppression. As the occult has become part of mainstream culture in America, the strongholds of the enemy have increased and multiplied.

We must pray in order to take ground. On our own, we are less powerful than the enemy, but when we pray, we can fight him successfully. We can march forward on our knees. The weapon he fears most is the weapon of prayer—which we should use "without ceasing" (1 Thessalonians 5:17 KJV).

Missionary statesman S. D. Gordon traveled to many of Satan's strongholds and gained a deep understanding of the vital power of prayer in spiritual warfare. He wrote,

> *In its simplest meaning, prayer has to do with conflict.*
> *Rightly understood it is the deciding factor in a spirit*
> *conflict. . . . Prayer is man giving God a footing on the*
> *contested territory of this earth.*[2]

Dick Eastman sees the importance of prayer in spiritual conflict as central. He writes, "Prayer is not so much another weapon on our list of weaponry as it is the actual battle."[3]

The Word Is the Sword

The Word of God gives us the strength to fight the devil in our personal lives. Remember that when Jesus was tempted by the devil, He fought him off by persistently quoting the Word of God (Matthew 4:1–11). The apostle John said the Word of God is what gives us strength to conquer.

> *I write to you, young men, because you are strong, and the word of God lives in you, and you have overcome the evil one.*
>
> 1 JOHN 2:14

Paul had trained himself to use the scriptures as an offensive weapon. He knew that nothing makes demons tremble like the sword of the Spirit, the Word of God.

> *Take the helmet of salvation and the sword of the Spirit, which is the word of God.*
>
> EPHESIANS 6:17

Daily Boot Camp

You cannot become a soldier without training. Learn to use your weapons. Every day set aside time to read, study, memorize, and apply the Word of God. Take time to pray urgent, faith-filled, passionate prayers. Become skilled in hearing and following the commands of your heavenly Commander. Surrender your cause for God's cause. As you do these things, you'll be known by the devil and his demons. You will give hell a headache.

Notes

1. Leonard Ravenhill, *Why Revival Tarries* (Minneapolis, MN: Bethany House Publishers, 1986), 186.
2. S. D. Gordon, *Quiet Talks on Prayer* (Grand Rapids, MI: Baker Book House, reprinted 1980), 31–38.
3. Dick Eastman, *Love On Its Knees* (Tarrytown, NY: Fleming Revel, 1989) p. 65.

5

Who Is My Neighbor?

Where are the Good Samaritans? I asked myself this question some time back when a newspaper blared this shocking headline: DETROIT CROWD CHEERS AS TRIO CHASE WOMAN TO HER DEATH. The story said,

> *As dozens of people looked on, and some cheered, three men pulled a woman from her car, ripped off her clothes, and chased her as she jumped or was forced off a bridge to her death. . . . None of the 40 or so passersby tried to help Deletha Word during the confrontation.*

The story went on to say that though nearly fifty people watched the awful events, "many of them were laughing about the men beating the woman." One person had a cellular phone, but would not call police. One witness said, "It seemed like people did not care."[1]

Lest we think a lack of compassion is a recent development, Jesus addressed the issue two thousand years ago. The Lord's words came in response to one man's dangerous question:

> *On one occasion an expert in the law stood up to test Jesus. "Teacher," he asked, "what must I do to inherit eternal life?"*
>
> *"What is written in the Law?" he replied. "How do you read it?"*

> *He answered: " 'Love the Lord your God with all your*
> *heart and with all your soul and with all your strength*
> *and with all your mind'; and, 'Love your neighbor as*
> *yourself.' "*
> *"You have answered correctly," Jesus replied. "Do this*
> *and you will live."*
> *But he wanted to justify himself, so he asked Jesus,*
> *"And **who is my neighbor?**"*
>
> LUKE 10:25–29

Who Is My Neighbor?

This religious leader was obviously rather selective in whom he chose to love, so he asked, "Who is my neighbor?" Jesus, a wonderful teacher, did not answer the question directly, but rather told a story—a story that more than answered the man's question.

> *"A man was going down from Jerusalem to Jericho, when*
> *he fell into the hands of robbers. They stripped him of*
> *his clothes, beat him and went away, leaving him half*
> *dead. A priest happened to be going down the same road,*
> *and when he saw the man, he passed by on the other*
> *side. So too, a Levite, when he came to the place and saw*
> *him, passed by on the other side. But a Samaritan, as he*
> *traveled, came where the man was; and when he saw him,*
> *he took pity on him. He went to him and bandaged his*
> *wounds, pouring on oil and wine. Then he put the man*
> *on his own donkey, took him to an inn and took care of*
> *him. The next day he took out two silver coins and gave*
> *them to the innkeeper. 'Look after him,' he said, 'and*
> *when I return, I will reimburse you for any extra expense*
> *you may have.'*

*"Which of these three do you think was a neighbor to
the man who fell into the hands of robbers?"*

*The expert in the law replied, "The one who had
mercy on him."*

Jesus told him, "Go and do likewise."

LUKE 10:30–37

The Priest

The first person who had a chance to help was not your
ordinary Joe—or should I say, Joseph. He was a priest, of
all people. Yet he passed by on the other side? That's bad.

But maybe the guy was busy. Maybe he was running
late for a meeting. Maybe he passed by because his plate was
already full of problems, and he didn't need another one right
then. This half-dead man would be a big problem. He'd need
time and attention, money and emotional energy.

Or maybe the priest was just playing it safe. He might have
sensed a trap. The wounded man could be a decoy with hidden
thieves nearby just waiting to pounce.

We don't know why he refused to help. We just know he
didn't help.

The Levite

It's interesting that the guy who asked the question about
loving our neighbors was a lawyer, possibly a Levite himself.
Levites were priests' assistants and were sometimes called
lawyers. From our modern perspective, we would think a
lawyer would certainly stop, if for no other reason than to file a
claim. "Sue the crooks who did this. Sue the people who built
this road in such a dangerous place. Sue the police for never

being there when you need them. This could be worth several million bucks."

But two thousand years ago in Israel, Levites and lawyers didn't concern themselves with civil, but religious, law. They saw that the rules of the Jews were explained and enforced. Certainly he'd stop, right?

Wrong.

The Samaritan

A Samaritan was a person from Samaria. They were racially mixed—half Jewish and half non-Jewish. Samaritans dated back to about 700 BC, around the time the Assyrian Empire overran Israel. The conquered Israelites forfeited their Jewish heritage, adopted some pagan worship practices, and intermarried with Gentiles who were sent into Samaria to repopulate the area. As such, the Samaritans were despised by the Jews.

No one would ever expect a Samaritan to stop to help a Jew. That would be like asking a runaway slave to help an injured slave owner in Mississippi in 1850. But the Samaritan of Jesus' story did something truly shocking:

> *"He took pity on him. He went to him and bandaged his wounds, pouring on oil and wine. Then he put the man on his own donkey, took him to an inn and took care of him. The next day he took out two silver coins and gave them to the innkeeper. 'Look after him,' he said, 'and when I return, I will reimburse you for any extra expense you may have.' "*

> LUKE 10:33–35

The Samaritan crossed racial and religious barriers to help the Jewish man. He took risks. He risked not only getting mugged himself, he risked having the victim reject his help because it came from a hated Samaritan. He risked his reputation with his Samaritan friends, who would probably take offense at him for helping a Jew.

The Samaritan gave up his time. How long do you think it took to stop, bandage the wounded Jew, and take him to an inn? The Samaritan inconvenienced himself. Who wants a dirty, bloody man messing up the back of his nice, clean donkey? Who wants to walk while a half-dead Jew rides his animal? Who wants to go that far out of his way for someone else?

Even beyond that, the Samaritan paid for the other man's stay and care at the inn. Those two silver coins weren't fifty cent pieces—they would be equivalent to about 250 dollars each. Imagine spending five hundred dollars to help a person you'd never even met.

The Samaritan could have said, "I've gone to all this cost and trouble, and I'll go no further. This is my limit." But no, he went as far as was needed. He volunteered to pay any extra expense necessary.

Wow! Put a big *S* on his chest for Superfriend.

Then, as He always did, Jesus asked the self-righteous lawyer a dangerous little question of his own.

> *"Which of these three do you think was a neighbor to the man who fell into the hands of robbers?"*
>
> *The expert in the law replied, "The one who had mercy on him."*
>
> *Jesus told him, "Go and do likewise."*
>
> LUKE 10:36–37

My Good Samaritan

I have a nasty little secret I need to confess. I don't like this story.

I think I've always had an aversion to the Good Samaritan. That guy is just too much. We're supposed to be like him, yet I often feel more like the priest or Levite. When it comes to that kind of compassion, I feel like a loser, a love bozo.

One night after everyone else in the house went to bed, I got honest with God. I said, "God, I hate this story. I've tried and I can never be like the Good Samaritan. What's wrong with me?"

It seemed like God was saying, "I know you don't quite live up to the profile of the Good Samaritan."

That's for sure, I thought.

"But you don't exactly fit the profile of the priest and Levite either. I've seen you get involved with hurting people. I've seen the time, the tears, and the money you've given to people in need."

Then it seemed like God was prompting me to look at the characters in this story again.

"Okay. There is the Samaritan, the priest, and the Levite."

"And. . . ?"

"And. . .there's the guy who got robbed and left for dead."

Then it hit me. I *am* in this story. Not so much as the priest or scribe, or even the Samaritan. I began to laugh. "I'm the half-dead guy."

Then I wondered, *Who's the Good Samaritan? No one has ever loved me like that? No one. . .*

It was as though God cleared His throat.

Then I understood. "No one ever loved me like that, except. . .Jesus. Jesus is the Good Samaritan. Jesus is *my* Good Samaritan."

Was I really half dead? According to the Bible, before we

meet Jesus, we are all dead in our sins (Ephesians 2:1). Our spirits are dead to God and the things of God.

Was I really that needy? The Bible describes us as being spiritually destitute (Revelation 3:17).

Was I really dirty? According to the scriptures, before being saved, we are unclean and all our righteousness is as filthy rags (Isaiah 64:6).

Was I really a foreigner? Prior to being adopted into God's forever family, we are aliens (Ephesians 2:19).

Was I really helpless and hopeless? According to the Bible, that is truly our spiritual condition apart from Christ (Ephesians 2:12).

I am that half-dead guy, beaten and dirty, left to die by the side of the road.

And so are you.

Religion can't help us. When we really need help most, religion will just walk on by. We need someone who is both willing and able to save us. We need a Good Samaritan, and God the Father sent one. Actually, something even better.

Like the Samaritan, Jesus crossed barriers. God became a man.

Like the Samaritan, He came to us when we could not get up to Him.

Like the Samaritan, He risked our rejection in order to meet our needs.

Like the Samaritan, He paid a great price for us. Unlike the Samaritan, the price He paid is not measurable in dollars and cents—He paid with His own life. He died to save us. He died loving us. He died to be our friend.

Better than the Samaritan, He didn't just bandage us up, He made us brand-new. He's not merely taking us to an inn, but one day he'll take us all the way home to His Father's mansion.

Instead of getting discouraged because you struggle to

be the Good Samaritan, be thankful that you *have* a Good Samaritan. You say, "But doesn't God want us to love like the Good Samaritan?" Absolutely! But be encouraged.

We can only begin to love *like* the Good Samaritan when we realize how much we have been loved *by* the Good Samaritan. We must continually grow in our awareness and appreciation of God's self-sacrificing love for us. As we do, we can become more and more like the Good Samaritan, and ultimately more like Jesus.

Notes

1. I read the article "Detroit Crowd Cheers as Trio Chase Woman to Her Death," in *The Columbus Dispatch*, August 22, 1995. More extensive coverage was available in an article by David Grant, "40 Watched Attackers Chase Woman to Her Death," *Detroit News*, August 21, 1995.

Why Have You Forsaken Me?

MATTHEW 27:46

I don't know what shadows may currently darken your life, but I want to remind you that Jesus is the light of the world. Maybe it feels as though you walk down a dark tunnel, but Jesus is the light at the end of the tunnel. Perhaps you're in a period of midnight gloom, but with Jesus, joy comes in the morning. He knows all about the darkness, and He knows all about *your* darkness.

Please walk back with me two thousand years.

Jesus and His disciples had finished their last meal together that fateful Thursday evening. During that special supper in the upper room, Jesus instituted the memorial meal commemorating His coming death on the cross for our sins. After dinner, the men quietly descended the stairs and made their way across the small Kidron Valley. Out of the city, they climbed the Mount of Olives to the dark Garden of Gethsemane.

Ironically, the name Gethsemane means "the crush"—as olives were crushed there to release their oil. It was in that garden the old olive trees witnessed Jesus being crushed by the weight of all that lay ahead. Here He gazed into the cup of His coming suffering and crucifixion. What He saw squeezed Him so brutally that His forehead erupted into rivulets of blood. Here Jesus sought His heavenly Father for the strength to continue in the awful, yet awesome, plan to redeem a sinful world.

As Jesus finished His prayer, the hillside suddenly blazed with torchlight. The serene silence was shattered by rough and anxious voices. Crowded around Jesus were the angry faces of soldiers, temple guards, and Jewish leaders, as well as the troubled visage of the betrayer, Judas himself. To them Jesus raised a question.

The Hour When Darkness Reigns

"Am I leading a rebellion, that you have come with swords and clubs? Every day I was with you in the temple courts, and you did not lay a hand on me. But this is your hour—when darkness reigns."

LUKE 22:52–53

Notice that last sentence: *But this is your hour—when darkness reigns.* What a sinister, yet lyrical, word picture. *The hour darkness reigns.* From the utterance of those words, an unstoppable series of history-making events was unleashed. Jesus was arrested and dragged through a series of illegal trials and kangaroo courts. He was brutally whipped, beaten, mocked, and rejected. All of that was merely the shadow leading up to the true darkness that was to come.

When Jesus allowed Himself to be nailed on the cross, He made a choice that produced the greatest darkness a single soul would ever know. It was as He hung on the cross that darkness ruled supreme.

Remember that Jesus did not begin in Bethlehem. He is God—and as God He has always existed in fellowship with His father.

In the beginning was the Word, and the Word was with God, and the Word was God. He was with God in the beginning.

JOHN 1:1–2

Yet when Jesus went to the cross, He took all of our sins with Him. So the sinless Son of God became sin. God is holy—totally separate from all sin. His nature demands that He must judge and turn His back on sin. So when our sin was poured out on the Son, the Father had to turn away. Imagine the anguish He felt. God had to turn his back on His own Son, Jesus Christ. When God, who is light, turned his back on Jesus, it created a darkness so severe it literally affected the earth.

> *From the sixth hour until the ninth hour darkness came over all the land.*
>
> MATTHEW 27:45

The sixth hour on the Hebrew clock is noon; the ninth hour would be three p.m. I have been in Jerusalem at that time and the sun is blazingly bright. The sandstone buildings are alive with sunlight.

But not that day!

That afternoon, darkness reigned. Heavy shadows spread like a thick curtain over the land. When the Father turned His back on the Son, the sun refused to shine. For three awful hours, the Son of God was separated from God the Father. He experienced hell for each of us as He bore our sins and received our judgment.

This was one of the most significant, history-altering, powerful moments the Earth ever witnessed. It was the hour darkness reigned.

At this defining moment, Jesus uttered one of the most amazing, important, agonizing, and dangerous questions ever spoken.

My God, My God, Why Have You Forsaken Me?

> *About the ninth hour Jesus cried out in a loud voice,*
> *"Eloi, Eloi, lama sabachthani?"—which means, "My*
> *God, my God, **why have you forsaken me?"***
>
> MATTHEW 27:46

Sadder words were never spoken.

Jesus was racked by physical anguish. He hung suspended between earth and space—alone, dying, betrayed by Judas, denied by Peter, forsaken by His disciples, mocked by the crowd, and attacked by demons. It was horrific.

All of which He could bear.

But now, as He hung in darkness, dying on the cross, He faced the only unbearable thing in the world—His Father had turned His back on Jesus.

On the cross, Christ became our sacrificial Lamb. God the Father placed all the sin of all the people who had lived, were living, or would ever live on Jesus Christ. Sin was poured out on Him like raw sewage. His pure and innocent soul was darkened—Jesus became sin for us.

> *God made him who had no sin to be sin for us, so that in*
> *him we might become the righteousness of God.*
>
> 2 CORINTHIANS 5:21

In an amazing, grotesque way, the sinless Son of God became the greatest sinner of all time. With that sin came the price of separation.

> *But your iniquities have separated you from your God;*
> *your sins have hidden his face from you, so that he will*
> *not hear.*
>
> ISAIAH 59:2

At that moment, as darkness reigned, Jesus was truly alone in the universe—more alone than any man has ever been. Not merely rejected by the crowds, betrayed by a disciple, denied by a friend, and abandoned by His students; Jesus was forsaken by God.

Read those last three words again slowly—*forsaken by God.* Those haunting, piercing words stand alone as the bleakest conceivable indictment. In those awful hours when darkness reigned, God the Father was forced to turn His back on God the Son. Eternal communion was broken. Eons of unbroken fellowship were severed.

Deep within His soul, Jesus cried out the most dramatic, the most desperate question ever uttered by human lips, "My God, my God, why have You forsaken me?" Imagine, for the only time in all of eternity, Jesus could not even call God His Father. The best He could say was "My God."

> *My God, My God, why have You forsaken me?*
> *What has happened?*
> *Where are You, God?*

In a sense, this question was actually a realization, a stunning statement, an astounding declaration, a shocking discovery, a desperate plea—

> *My God, I am separated from You!*
> *It is too much. I cannot bear this.*
> *This darkness of separation is too much.*

It Was the Lord's Will to Crush Him

Seven hundred years earlier, this ghastly moment was predicted by the prophet Isaiah. He wrote:

*We all, like sheep, have gone astray, each of us has turned
to his own way; and the LORD has laid on him the
iniquity of us all.*

ISAIAH 53:6

*Yet it was the LORD's will to crush him and cause him to
suffer.*

ISAIAH 53:10

It is one thing to suffer at the hands of wicked men.
It is worse to be betrayed and abandoned by friends.
It is terrible to suffer at the hands of Satan.

But it is an entirely different thing to suffer at the hands
of your God. . .and Father.

At that moment on the cross, when Jesus asked, "Why
have You forsaken Me?", God the Father was crushing His
Son. The intensity, severity, and agony of such pain would have
been incalculable.

The author of Hebrews reminds us of a supremely somber
reality.

It is a dreadful thing to fall into the hands of the living God.

HEBREWS 10:31

Never before had darkness reigned over the earth in such
a great way.

Never before had darkness ruled over one soul in such a
great way.

God the Father allowed darkness to have dominion over
the soul of God the Son.

Why?

Why did God allow darkness to reign?

Why did God allow Jesus to fall into the hands of dark-
hearted men?

Why did God allow Jesus to be attacked by Satan?
Why did God allow Jesus to be separated from Himself?
Why did God forsake His Son?
Why?

Darkness Was Allowed to Reign Briefly in Order That Light May Reign Eternally

Read these verses slowly and seriously. Drink in the depth of love they proclaim.

> *For Christ died for sins once for all, the righteous for the unrighteous, to bring you to God.*
>
> 1 PETER 3:18

> *"For God so loved the world that he gave his one and only Son, that whoever believes in him shall not perish but have eternal life."*
>
> JOHN 3:16

> *"I am the light of the world."*
>
> JOHN 8:12

Remember, darkness reigned for hours; light reigns for eternity.

That Friday afternoon was shrouded in deep darkness. But three days later, life erupted from the grave, and the light of the world shone brilliantly.

Yes, the horrors of hell won briefly, but only in order that the gates of heaven could be opened wide. The devil claimed a victory that afternoon, but only so Jesus could win victory forever. Sin stood as champion over one so salvation could come to all. Death was king for a moment so life could be offered eternally.

Jesus experienced the greatest levels of darkness so we can experience the greatest levels of light.

Darkness only lasts through the night, but joy comes in the morning.

Jesus understands your pain.

Jesus Understands Your Pain and Has Defeated Your Darkness

Maybe it feels as though God has forsaken you. Maybe you are experiencing the frightening loneliness of a seemingly passive silence from the sovereign God.

Maybe the vultures of darkness are circling your soul. The terrors of terrible trials have ravaged your faith.

Maybe you feel lost in a wilderness of darkness and wonder when, if ever, you will find the way out.

Are you struggling with some dark situation in your life? Maybe a loved one is in the hospital—or has died. Maybe it's a personal health issue. It could be a job. There might be an unexplained, unresolved hurt. Possibly there is a dark cloud turning everything you see to gloom.

Cry out to Jesus.

He understands.

He cares.

Come to the Lord of Light. He can chase all your darkness away.

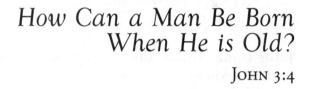

How Can a Man Be Born When He is Old?

JOHN 3:4

"Lose Your Religion!"

A few years ago, my church mailed out ten thousand postcards emblazoned with the words, "Lose Your Religion!" On the back of the card, I paraphrased the words of Jesus, "If all you have is religion, you will never see the kingdom of heaven" (John 3:3). I also paraphrased the words of the apostle Paul, who said that "religion is dung" (Philippians 3:3–10).

As I had expected, we received some very interesting e-mails that week. People wanted to know how I, as the pastor of a well-known church, could be so dead set against religion.

My point was simple: Religion by itself is not enough. Religion will not get anyone to heaven. Real Christianity is a *relationship*. It is a relationship into which you must be spiritually born. You must be born again.

Nic at Night

Nicodemus hoped his clandestine meeting would go unnoticed in the clamor of the Passover celebration. Power, position, prestige—he potentially had much to lose. Meeting with Jesus, the unsanctioned teacher, could cost Nicodemus dearly.

Nicodemus was not merely a Pharisee. He was a member

of the Sanhedrin, the elite group of seventy men who ruled Israel in all matters regarding religion. Religion—that's what had raised his curiosity about Jesus. It seems Jesus was more committed to talking about a relationship with God than about keeping religious rituals and rules. The miracles Jesus had performed had piqued Nicodemus's interest to see if this man really was who some said He was—the Messiah.

So Nicodemus came at night and sat down across from Jesus. Peter, James, and John probably sat in the background, joined by a few of Nicodemus's assistants. They may have been surprised by the unthreatening manner with which Nicodemus approached Jesus. But Nicodemus was soul thirsty. Jesus wisely whetted his appetite and drew from his lips a most dangerous question.

> *Now there was a man of the Pharisees named Nicodemus, a member of the Jewish ruling council. He came to Jesus at night and said, "Rabbi, we know you are a teacher who has come from God. For no one could perform the miraculous signs you are doing if God were not with him."*
>
> *In reply Jesus declared, "I tell you the truth, no one can see the kingdom of God unless he is born again."*
>
> ***"How can a man be born when he is old?"*** *Nicodemus asked. "Surely he cannot enter a second time into his mother's womb to be born!"*
>
> JOHN 3:1–4

"How Can a Man Be Born When He Is Old?"

Jesus had said no one could even *see* heaven without being born again. But Nicodemus wasn't sure what it meant to be "born again." He knew that a second physical birth made no sense. So Jesus explained.

Jesus answered, "I tell you the truth, no one can enter the kingdom of God unless he is born of water and the Spirit. Flesh gives birth to flesh, but the Spirit gives birth to spirit. You should not be surprised at my saying, 'You must be born again.' The wind blows wherever it pleases. You hear its sound, but you cannot tell where it comes from or where it is going. So it is with everyone born of the Spirit."

JOHN 3:5–8

Religion Is Not Good Enough

Sometimes it's easier to understand what a person is saying by first determining what he or she is *not* saying. Clearly, Jesus was not saying that people needed to be very religious to enter the kingdom of heaven. Nicodemus did not need to become religious because he already was very religious. As we read in John 3:1, he was "a member of the Jewish ruling council."

In order to be on that select council of seventy, one had to be a Pharisee. Pharisees were the most religious of the Jews. Their whole life was religion. The word *Pharisee* is from a word meaning "separate." The Pharisees were noted as those who kept away from anyone or anything they considered to be religiously unclean. They fasted two days every week and never missed synagogue. The Pharisees felt the Old Testament had too *few* religious rules in it, so they added hundreds of their own.

But Nicodemus was more than a Pharisee—he was a leader of the Pharisees! He was a part of the ruling council known as the Sanhedrin. These seventy men were the most religious of the Pharisees.

If anyone was religious, it was Nicodemus. Yet his religion was not good enough. Jesus looked Nicodemus in the eye and told him that he had to be born again. That must have been a little unnerving for Nicodemus—if his religion wasn't good enough, whose would be? Would yours?

Recently I asked a man this question: "If you died today, are you certain you would be welcomed into heaven?"

He said, "I guess so."

I asked him, "On what basis would God let you in?"

He replied, "Well, I go to church."

I asked, "If I sat in a garage a few hours every week, would it make me a car?"

He laughed and said, "Of course not."

So I replied, "Sitting in a garage will no more make you a car than attending a church will make you a Christian. Jesus said that you need to be born again."

Being Good Is Not Good Enough

Not long ago, I asked a young lady the question, "If you died today, are you certain you would be welcomed into heaven?", and the follow up question, "On what basis would God let you into heaven?"

She answered, "I'm a pretty good person."

"But are you good enough?" I asked.

She didn't care much for that question, answering with a certain amount of pride, "Well, I'm better than most."

"But is that good enough?" I pressed. "Is your righteousness good enough to get you into heaven?"

She answered, "I hope so. . .I don't know. What *is* good enough?"

"According to the Bible," I replied, "the only righteousness that is good enough for heaven is perfection. Are you perfect?"

"No."

"Then maybe your righteousness is not good enough. Jesus said that you need to be born again."

The Bible teaches that there has been only one person in history who was "good enough." Only one person hit the bull's-eye of the righteousness required by God. That person is Jesus Christ. He is the only one who earned a relationship with a perfect God by living a sinless life. Yet He died in our place on the cross and rose again from the dead. So our relationship with God is not the result of the religion we have or good works we do. It is the result of believing in what Jesus has *done*. It is not something we earn. It's a gift we receive.

You see, if we could get to heaven by being really religious or really good, why did Jesus have to die for sin? No matter how good we are, we are not perfect. No matter how much good we do, we can't erase the stain of our past sins.

A Second Birth

Being born again is not something you do. It's something you experience. Jesus was crystal clear: You will not experience the kingdom of God unless you experience a second birth.

I asked a gentleman if he was born again. He told me, "Sure, I've been a Christian all my life." That's not what Jesus was saying. He said we need a *second* birth. We need to be born *again*.

A Spiritual Birth

Nicodemus was thinking in physical terms when he asked:

> *"How can a man be born when he is old? . . .Surely he cannot enter a second time into his mother's womb to be born!"*
>
> JOHN 3:4

Jesus responded that being "born again" is experiencing a *spiritual* birth.

> *Jesus answered, "I tell you the truth, no one can enter the kingdom of God unless he is born of water and the Spirit. Flesh gives birth to flesh, but the Spirit gives birth to spirit."*
>
> JOHN 3:5–6

By describing births of both water *and* the Spirit, Jesus contrasted physical birth with spiritual birth. He said we need both.

It was the physical birth Jesus described in verse 5 when he said "born of water." When a woman is pregnant, a sack of water protects the baby inside her. She knows the baby is ready to come when the water breaks. When the baby is born, it's all wet—because the physical birth involves being "born of water."

By saying, "Flesh gives birth to flesh," Jesus was further referring to physical birth. When we are born physically, we mark the event with a certificate that gives the date, time, and place of our arrival. Note carefully that Jesus said the physical birth alone will not get us into the kingdom of God. We need a spiritual birth. We need to be "born of water *and* the Spirit" (John 3:5).

The First Birth Is Not Good Enough

I once saw a bumper sticker that said, "Born once. It was good enough." I thought, *Not according to Jesus.* Jesus taught the first birth is insufficient. Our first birth is corrupted by our sin nature, called "the flesh."

"The Spirit gives life; the flesh counts for nothing."

JOHN 6:63

I know that nothing good lives in me, that is, in my sinful nature. For I have the desire to do what is good, but I cannot carry it out.

ROMANS 7:18

"So, How Do I Get Born Again?"

One day, a lady became upset with me because I had mentioned the fact that we are all sinners.

"Sinner?" she said. "That is such a strong term. I resent being called a sinner."

I asked her, "How many murders does it take to be a murderer?"

"One," she replied. "It only takes one."

"So," I continued, "how many sins does it take to be a sinner?"

"Oh," she said. "Now I see what you mean. So, how do I get born again?"

The answer is given later in Jesus' discussion with Nicodemus.

"For God so loved the world that he gave his one and only Son, that whoever believes in him shall not perish but have eternal life."

JOHN 3:16

John's Gospel also says,

Yet to all who received him [Jesus], to those who believed in his name, he gave the right to become children of God [i.e., be born again].

JOHN 1:12

We are born again when, by faith, we receive Jesus Christ as our savior.

Let me ask several vitally important questions:

1. Do you know the date, time, and place of your spiritual birth?
2. Do you know for sure that you have been born again?
3. If you are not absolutely certain that you have been born again, will you respond to God and be born again today, on this date, at this time, at this place? This is a chance to make sure.

Below is a simple prayer hundreds have prayed when they were serious about turning their lives over to Jesus Christ. Read through it. If you mean it, you can say it to God.

Dear God,

I admit that I have sinned. I admit that my religion alone is not going to give me a relationship with You. I admit that my goodness is not good enough. I admit that I need to be born again.

I believe that Jesus is God's Son. I believe that Jesus never sinned. I believe that Jesus died to pay for my sins. I believe that Jesus rose from the dead to give me eternal life.

Right now, I call upon the name of the Lord Jesus to save me. I ask the Holy Spirit to come into my heart and make me a new person. I ask that I may be born again as a child of God. I surrender the throne of my heart to You. I ask to experience Your love and power.

I am willing to do anything You tell me to do. I am willing to stop doing anything that displeases You. I ask for the power to follow You all the days of my life.

In Jesus' name, amen.

If you said that prayer to God and meant it, you might want to fill out the spiritual birth certificate below. Also, please send me an e-mail (dbearley@liberty.edu) so I can rejoice with you and pray for you.

My Spiritual Birth Certificate

On _____ _____, 20____,

I, _____ _____,

was born again by responding to God's Word
and called upon the name of the Lord to save me.
I am now born again as I have admitted my sin,
believed in Jesus Christ to pay for my sin,
and committed my life to Him.

Which Is the Greatest Commandment?

MATTHEW 22:36

What really matters? What are the most important things in life?

One way to choose your top priorities is to consider what you want people to say about you at your funeral. Epitaphs are brief statements commemorating or epitomizing a deceased person. They can be spoken or written. Some are serious; others are not. In years past, they were often written on gravestones. Following are some of the best I've either seen or read about.

In a Uniontown, Pennsylvania, cemetery, one gravestone tells the story of an accident:

*Here lies the body
of Jonathan Blake.
Stepped on the gas
instead of the brake.*

A headstone in a Silver City, Nevada, cemetery tells of a gun battle:

*Here lays Butch,
We planted him raw.
He was quick on the trigger,
But slow on the draw.*

In the Boot Hill Cemetery in Tombstone, Arizona:

Here lies Lester Moore
Four slugs from a .44
No Les No More

Anna Hopewell's gravestone in Enosburg Falls, Vermont, is amusing:

Here lies the body of our Anna,
Done to death by a banana.
It wasn't the fruit that laid her low,
But the skin of the thing that made her go.

Some epitaphs don't rhyme. On Margaret Daniels' grave at Hollywood Cemetery in Richmond, Virginia, we read:

She always said her feet were killing her
But nobody believed her.

A headstone in a London cemetery reads,

Here lies Ann Mann,
Who lived an old maid
But died an old Mann.
Dec. 8, 1767

In a Thurmont, Maryland, cemetery is this thought-provoker:

Here lies an Atheist
All dressed up
And no place to go.

My favorite was one we saw on vacation at a cemetery in

Key West, Florida. It simply says:

I Told You I Was Sick

Those are all pretty funny. But the very best headstone I'm aware of honored a man whose life made a positive difference. Dr. John Geddie went to the Pacific island of Aneiteum in 1848 as a missionary and worked there for God for twenty-four years. On the tablet erected to his memory, these words were inscribed:

When he landed, in 1848, there were no Christians.
When he left, in 1872, there were no heathen.[1]

What would the epitaph of your life be? Several years ago, a friend of mine was diagnosed with cancer. When he died soon thereafter, his family held a service celebrating his life. Relatives and friends shared the positive impact he had had on their lives. They talked about his unswerving commitment to God, his deep love of his family, and his effect on others. After that night, I determined to make sure I knew what was most important—and to spend the rest of my life living for what mattered most.

A Dangerous Question for Jesus

Jesus had become an annoying irritant and potentially large threat to the business-as-usual religion of the Pharisees. His teachings and lifestyle exposed the superficial character of their legalistic rituals and manmade rules. He spoke of life and love. He talked about a genuine relationship with God. He was refreshingly authentic and had a passionate depth and compassionate heart that drew people to Him.

Since their religion was built on words and rules, the Pharisees tried to discredit Jesus by trapping him in the web of questions and theoretical dilemmas. They asked, "Is it right for a Jew to pay taxes?" and "In the resurrection who will be the husband of a remarried widow?" But Jesus was no fool. He repeatedly avoided their rhetorical knots and tied them up in their own questions.

Finally, they came at Him with an apparently unsolvable dilemma. The question was simple, presumably unanswerable, and designed to discredit Jesus. It went like this: "Out of the 613 commands given in the Old Testament law, which was the greatest?" The Pharisees figured that if Jesus named one command as greater than another, He would be disparaging the rest. Then they would nail Him for dealing irreverently with the Word of God.

> *Hearing that Jesus had silenced the Sadducees, the Pharisees got together. One of them, an expert in the law, tested him with this question:*
> *"Teacher,* **which is the greatest commandment** *in the Law?"*
>
> MATTHEW 22:34–36

This attempted trap serves as one of the most dangerous questions in the Bible. It was potentially dangerous then, as to answer incorrectly would discredit Jesus as a teacher. It is dangerous now, as the way we answer it and what we do with it will change our lives.

Notice the amazing wisdom of Jesus as He skillfully answered their dilemma.

> *Jesus replied: " 'Love the Lord your God with all your heart and with all your soul and with all your mind.' This is the first and greatest commandment. And the second is*

*like it: 'Love your neighbor as yourself.' All the Law and
the Prophets hang on these two commandments."*

MATTHEW 22:37–40

Jesus' reply is marvelous. He cut to the main point of the
commandments by quoting two passages, one from the sixth
chapter of Deuteronomy, the other from an obscure corner
of Leviticus 19. That concisely, Jesus summarized the 613
commands of the Old Testament law (plus those of the rest of
the entire Bible) and simplified all of life at the same time. His
answer? "Love God and love people—everything else hangs off
those two pegs."

Do you see the brilliance of Jesus' answer? Instead of
giving the Pharisees a loophole that allowed them to obey
one commandment while ignoring another, He gave them
one commandment that contained all the commandments of
God in two simple sentences: "Love the Lord" and "Love your
neighbor."

Priorities

Priority can be defined as "something given precedence of rank
in terms of time, energy, thought, finances, etc." A priority is
something that is valued or deemed as important. We often
state what is important to us by how we spend our time
and money. I have learned there are several truths regarding
priorities:

1. Not everything can be a priority.

You cannot have it all. The commercials say you can, but don't
believe them. We are not infinite beings. None of us can have
it all or do it all. When we try to do so, we become overloaded
and overwhelmed.

2. *Not everything should be a priority.*

Not all things are created equal. Not every activity is the best choice possible. We must choose when it comes to priorities. Some activities and investments are more important than others.

3. *Fulfilling two commands must become our priorities.*

Jesus summarized life's most important priorities and simplified life for us into one awesome statement—love God and love people. Notice what Jesus did *not* give as being of primary importance: things, achievements, careers, and money. He did not list possessions, power, popularity, pets, pleasure, comfort, convenience, entertainment, or recreation as having chief importance, either.

Loving God

Loving God is a choice. The verse Jesus quoted, "Love the LORD your God" (Deuteronomy 6:5), was originally written in Hebrew. The Hebrew term translated "love" describes an act of the will characterized by dedication and commitment of choice. Matthew's Gospel was written in Greek. The Greek term used here for "love" is the verb of intelligent, purposeful, committed love. Both languages make it clear that loving God is a choice. This is also evident by the fact that loving God is used as an imperative (or command) in this verse. Loving God is more than a random feeling or an innate urge. It is a choice that must be made.

Choosing to Love God Above Everything Else

Early in high school, I felt I could balance my life by segregating parts of it into separate boxes. I had a big box for

sports, a container for friends, and a section for school. I had
separate boxes for art, music, my paper route, family, and God.
I was central in my life and my boxes revolved around me.

God was definitely part of my life, but only in His own
box. I went to church on Sunday, and I helped a friend with a
ministry to poor children. I got my "God box" out if something
really bad happened. But besides that, I kept God in His box.
I was reluctant to allow Him to affect the other areas of my life.
I really loved God with only half a heart—or less.

I was miserable.

For a couple of years, I disobeyed the Great Commandment
as I battled to be the center of my own life, keeping God in
His own box. Eventually, I tired of the mess I was making.
I felt so empty. My friends who loved God with all of their
hearts were full of joy. They seemed so much more happy and
satisfied. I thirsted for that type of relationship with God.

One Sunday morning, I delivered my newspapers and went
to church. As usual, I went to the very last row of the balcony,
to the corner farthest from the platform. Normally, when the
sermon would start, I would fall asleep. But that Sunday was
different. Someone had handed me a bulletin on the way in,
and that piece of paper had a large boxed quote that read:

> *Commitment to God is simply giving all you know of
> yourself to all you know of God.*

I was intrigued. *I can do that,* I thought. *I can't be perfect
or spiritual on my own. I have tried so many times and failed
miserably. I have tried the overly emotional route, and that did
not last. But I can choose to give all I know of myself to all I know
of God.*

I have no recollection of that day's sermon. All I could
think about was, "Commitment to God is simply giving all
you know of yourself to all you know of God."

Later that night, at the invitation of a friend, I attended a student gathering held in a large house. As dozens of teens sang praise to God and gave testimonies of His work in their lives, I could only think of one thing: "Commitment to God is simply giving all you know of yourself to all you know of God."

At home that night, I went straight to my room and got down on my knees. My prayer was simple.

> *God, I believe You are real.*
>
> *I am very sorry for my sins and the mess I have been making of my life.*
>
> *As of this moment, by an act of my will, I choose to give all I know of me to all I know of You.*
>
> *From this moment on I choose to put You ahead of sports, friends, school, art, music, my paper route, and my family. No more boxes. You can have all of me—past, present, and future.*
>
> *I want to put You first and love You most.*
>
> *Amen.*

I did not hear thunder or see lightning. But for the first time in a long time, I experienced inner fullness, deep peace, and an especially rich joy. I felt clean and whole, loved and accepted.

Choosing to love God above all else is a commitment I must return to consistently. Sometimes it's easy—because I know that God is perfect, wise, powerful, and good. But other times, choosing to love God is excruciatingly difficult. My own desires can draw me away. God's discipline is sometimes hard to accept. At times, He seems silent. But my priority is to love Him.

Choosing to Really Love People

The second half of the great command is loving people as much as we love ourselves. That can be a challenge—because people are flawed, imperfect, needy beings. Loving people is hard when they can't (or worse, they refuse) to return our love. It's hard when they hurt us.

But we must remember this: Loving people is a choice to be made and a command to be obeyed before it becomes a feeling to be felt. The feeling may come or it might never come. But we must still act in love.

Jesus elaborated on what He meant by "loving our neighbors" when He gave His famous teaching on the mountainside. Slowly read His words below. As you do, realize that the only way you can love this way is by focusing on the love God has already given you.

> *"To you who are ready for the truth, I say this: Love your enemies. Let them bring out the best in you, not the worst. When someone gives you a hard time, respond with the energies of prayer for that person. If someone slaps you in the face, stand there and take it. If someone grabs your shirt, giftwrap your best coat and make a present of it. If someone takes unfair advantage of you, use the occasion to practice the servant life. No more tit-for-tat stuff. Live generously.*
>
> *"Here is a simple rule of thumb for behavior: Ask yourself what you want people to do for you; then grab the initiative and do it for them! If you only love the lovable, do you expect a pat on the back? Run-of-the-mill sinners do that. If you only help those who help you, do you expect a medal? Garden-variety sinners do that. If you only give for what you hope to get out of it, do you think that's charity? The stingiest of pawnbrokers does that.*

"I tell you, love your enemies. Help and give without expecting a return. You'll never—I promise—regret it. Live out this God-created identity the way our Father lives toward us, generously and graciously, even when we're at our worst. Our Father is kind; you be kind.

"Don't pick on people, jump on their failures, criticize their faults—unless, of course, you want the same treatment. Don't condemn those who are down; that hardness can boomerang. Be easy on people; you'll find life a lot easier. Give away your life; you'll find life given back, but not merely given back—given back with bonus and blessing. Giving, not getting, is the way. Generosity begets generosity."

LUKE 6:27–38 THE MESSAGE

Thank God that He has consistently loved you with this type of love. Ask God to help you love the people you will meet today in the same ways He has loved you.

Notes

1. "Influence," Sermon Illustrations.com, http://www.sermonillustrations .com/a-z/i/influence.htm (accessed June 20, 2007).

Will You Really Lay Down Your Life for Me?

JOHN 13:38

It was an important night in Jerusalem. The disciples were gathered together with Jesus in an upper room for a meal. It would be the last supper they would share before Jesus would be arrested, tried, beaten, crucified, and resurrected. Judas had just left to set into motion the ugly events that rested ominously on the horizon. Jesus commented that He would be with the disciples only a little longer. He also said that they could not come where He was going (John 13:33). Peter, feeling secure in his role as lead disciple, began to ask Jesus questions. Unknowingly, it would lead Jesus to ask him, and the rest of us, a most dangerous question.

Will You Really Lay Down Your Life for Me?

> *Simon Peter asked him, "Lord, where are you going?"*
> *Jesus replied, "Where I am going, you cannot follow now, but you will follow later."*
> *Peter asked, "Lord, why can't I follow you now? I will lay down my life for you."*
> *Then Jesus answered, **"Will you really lay down your life for me?"***
>
> JOHN 13:36–38

Following the way of Jesus was (and is) radically serious business. It is a path littered with life-and-death implications. Knowing his death was imminent, Jesus had given strong hints that true discipleship was a difficult road leading to sacrifice—even death.

> *"If anyone would come after me, he must deny himself and take up his cross daily and follow me. For whoever wants to save his life will lose it, but whoever loses his life for me will save it."*
>
> LUKE 9:23–24

> *"If anyone comes to me and does not hate his father and mother, his wife and children, his brothers and sisters—yes, even his own life—he cannot be my disciple. And anyone who does not carry his cross and follow me cannot be my disciple."*
>
> LUKE 14:26–27

Earlier that very week, Jesus had clearly said that His life was to be like a seed that must die in the ground before bearing much fruit. His way was leading to His death. To follow Him was to take the same path with the same outcome:

> *"I tell you the truth, unless a kernel of wheat falls to the ground and dies, it remains only a single seed. But if it dies, it produces many seeds. The man who loves his life will lose it, while the man who hates his life in this world will keep it for eternal life. Whoever serves me must follow me; and where I am, my servant also will be. My Father will honor the one who serves me."*
>
> JOHN 12:24–26

Peter was quite confident that he could handle the painful path of sacrifice Jesus was leading them down. Boldly he declared, "I will lay down my life for you" (John 13:37).

But Jesus knew Peter. Without truly coming to the end of himself, he would never learn how to rely on Jesus when facing the option of denial or death. So Jesus asked Peter a most dangerous question, followed by a disheartening prediction.

> *"Will you really lay down your life for me? I tell you the truth, before the rooster crows, you will disown me three times!"*
>
> JOHN 13:38

As we know, Jesus was right. Later that awful night, Peter did deny Jesus three times (Luke 22:54–61). Peter's failure broke his heart. He lost his arrogance and his pride died. When he realized what he had done, he wept bitter tears of remorse (Luke 22:62). Fortunately for Peter, God gives second chances and new life. Fortunately for Peter, he allowed his failure to create in him greater dependence upon Christ. He became the bold preacher of Pentecost (Acts 2) and a man willing to face imprisonment and beating for Jesus (Acts 4, 12).

Would Peter really lay down his life for Jesus? History tells us that he ultimately answered yes. Rather than deny Jesus, Peter died with a glorious testimony as he was crucified upside down because of his faith in Christ.

He Said No

As we also know, one of Jesus' disciples refused to take the narrow way of sacrifice. When faced with the question of whether he would lay down his life for Christ, Judas answered no. Judas betrayed Jesus to the authorities for a bag of money.

Later, instead of repentance, he felt only a depressing remorse. Ironically, by trying to save his life, he died inside. Judas's guilt and shame ultimately led to his suicide.

They Answered Yes

Here are Jesus' last words before ascending into heaven:

> *"But you will receive power when the Holy Spirit comes on you; and you will be my witnesses in Jerusalem, and in all Judea and Samaria, and to the ends of the earth."*

Acts 1:8

It is interesting to note that the word *witness* is the same Greek word from which we get our word *martyr*. Jesus knew that taking the gospel to the world would be costly and that many would pay the ultimate price.

He was right.

Peter was not the only Christ-follower required to answer the question, "Will you really lay down your life for me?" History tells us that many said yes. Thousands died for their faith during the early years of the church.

A deacon named Stephen was preaching the gospel in Jerusalem on the Passover after Christ's crucifixion. He was cast out of the city and stoned to death (Acts 6–8). James, the son of Zebedee and the elder brother of John, was killed when Herod Agrippa I arrived as governor of Judea (Acts 12). History tells us that Philip suffered martyrdom at Hierapolis in Phrygia. He was scourged, thrown into prison, and afterwards crucified around AD 54.

Matthew, the tax collector from Capernaum who wrote a Gospel in Hebrew, was preaching in Ethiopia when he suffered martyrdom by the sword around AD 60. Andrew, the brother of Peter, preached the gospel throughout Asia. On his arrival at Edessa, he was arrested and crucified on a cross, two ends of which were fixed transversely in the ground (thus the term *St. Andrew's cross*). Bartholomew translated the Gospel of Matthew in India. He was cruelly beaten and crucified. Thomas, the one-time doubter of Christ, preached in Parthia and India. He was martyred with a spear.

James, the half brother of Jesus, led the church in Jerusalem and was the author of a book in the Bible. At the age of ninety-four he was beaten and stoned, and finally had his brains bashed out with a fuller's club. Matthias was the apostle who filled the vacant place of Judas. He was stoned at Jerusalem and then beheaded. Mark was converted to Christianity by Peter and then transcribed Peter's account of Jesus in his Gospel. Mark was dragged to pieces by the people of Alexandria in front of Serapis, their pagan idol.[1]

They Also Said Yes

Others with names less familiar were also martyred by heathen emperors, governors, and judges for refusing to denounce Jesus Christ. In his *Ecclesiastical History*, Eusebius tells of numerous martyrs in the Christian church prior to AD 324.[2]

They did not receive proper trials. Many were tortured before being put to death. Even as they suffered such abuse, they refused to deny Jesus. Picture the fearless faith in Christ of these few:

A man named Alpheus was scourged, scraped with iron hooks, and tortured on the rack, and eventually was beheaded.

A woman named Ennathas was scourged with thongs of hide. She endured the torture cheerfully, and when returned to the judge was condemned to the flames.

Metra was an old man who refused to deny Christ. His

tormentors beat his aged body with clubs then led him out of town where they stoned him to death.

Sanctus suffered unimaginable abuse. He was beaten, had hot brass plates attached to parts of his body, was scourged with a whip, and dragged down a road. When he survived the attacks of wild animals, his persecutors strapped him into an iron chair and roasted his body.

Still Saying Yes

The accounts of Christian martyrdom are not merely stories from antiquity. Tens of thousands die for Jesus each year. Many of their stories are untold, but here are two:

Three teenage girls in Poso, Central Sulawesi, Indonesia, all members of a Christian high school, were beheaded on October 29, 2005, by machete-wielding men dressed in black. One of the severed heads was placed in front of a church.[3]

In south India, Pastor Daniel and his wife, Hephzibah, started a Christian church in the Hyderabad area by distributing tracts. He was opposed and beaten several times, and finally on May 19, 2005, he disappeared, only to be found murdered a few days later. When Hephzibah went to identify Daniel's body, she could only recognize him by the clothes he'd been wearing. Acid had been poured over his body.[4]

She Said Yes

On Tuesday, April 20, 1999, seventeen-year-old Cassie Bernall was reading her Bible in the Columbine school library when two students burst in with guns. According to a witness, one of the killers pointed his weapon at Cassie and asked, "Do you believe in God?"

Another student in the library recalled what happened next:

She paused, like she didn't know what she was going to answer. . .then she said "yes." She must have been scared, but her voice didn't sound shaky. It was strong. Then they asked her why, though they didn't give her a chance to respond. They just blew her away.[5]

Will I Really Lay Down My Life for Christ?

This is a dangerous life-and-death question. I find it intensely challenging and deeply convicting. I read the accounts of these martyrs, and I ask myself, "Could I die for the One who died for me?" I don't know for sure. I hope I'd say yes. I like to believe He will give me the grace I will need if I ever face that awesome choice.

One thing I know for sure: If you and I are not living all of our lives for God now, we probably wouldn't die for Him then.

Notes

1. "Christian Persecution: Dramatic Evidence," All About Following Jesus, http://www.allaboutfollowingjesus.org/christian-persecution.htm (accessed June 20, 2007).
2. Eusebius, *Ecclesiastical History,* http://www.innvista.com/culture/religion/earlmart.htm (accessed June 20, 2007).
3. *Witness Magazine,* July 2006, "Pray That God Would Restrain Militants," http://www.releaseinternational.org/media/download_gallery/wit29web.pdf (accessed June 20, 2007).
4. *Witness Magazine,* July 2006, "On the March," http://www.releaseinternational.org/media/Witness/wit32web.pdf (accessed June 20, 2007).

5. Misty Bernall, *She Said Yes!* (New York: Pocket Books, 1999), 14. The so-called myth of Cassie's shooting is debunked in the *Christianity Today* article, "Cassie Said Yes, They Said No" by Wendy Murray Zoba, http://ctlibrary.com/14911, November 1, 1999 (accessed June 20, 2007).

Did God Really Say. . . ?

GENESIS 3:1

Have you ever been less-than-convinced of something God has said in His Word? Have you ever had questions about the validity, reliability, and authority of God's Word? Have you ever used your skepticism as an excuse for disobedience? If so, you are not the first.

Did God Really Say. . . ?

The story of the Bible opens with what may be the most dangerous question of them all. It is a question that can potentially render the rest of the Bible meaningless.

In the beginning, God did not give Adam hundreds of pages of rules. In fact, there was only one very simple rule: *Don't eat the fruit of the tree of the knowledge of good and evil.* Other than that, Adam, do as you please.

> *And the LORD God commanded the man, "You are free to eat from any tree in the garden; but you must not eat from the tree of the knowledge of good and evil, for when you eat of it you will surely die."*
>
> GENESIS 2:16–17

It was a simple enough command: "Don't eat the fruit of this one tree." The consequences were clearly explained: "If you disobey, you will die." It should have been easy enough to obey. The garden was loaded with plenty of trees bearing an abundant supply of wonderful fruit. Adam and Eve would not need to eat from the forbidden tree. No problem.

But then a cloud appeared on the horizon. It was the cloud of doubt surrounding one of the most dangerous questions ever asked. You know the story:

> *Now the serpent was more crafty than any of the wild animals the LORD God had made. He said to the woman, "**Did God really say,** 'You must not eat from any tree in the garden'?"*
>
> GENESIS 3:1

Sure, on the surface it seems like a simple enough question. It opens with four apparently innocent words: "Did God really say?" But underneath the serpent's slick smile and false ignorance lies sinister intent. Those four words raise dangerous uncertainty about the authority of the Word of God. Suspicion is aroused about the goodness of God. The command of God is questioned. Most damaging is that the question "smuggles in the assumption that God's word is subject to our judgment."[1]

The rest of the story is familiar. Adam and Eve doubted the Word of God, and as a result, they disregarded God's one simple command (Genesis 3:2–6). It was not only a watershed moment in *their* lives, it was also one of the defining moments in all human history. Adam and Eve's disobedience led to disastrous results and dragged the entire planet down with them. Doubt can be dangerous to us and damaging to others when we give in and disregard the Word of God. But doubt can also be dangerous to the enemy when it leads us to greater faith.

Is the Bible the Word of God?

I put the question on the search engine Google. The very first article listed was from a Web site hosted by the "Internet Infidels" who arrogantly describe themselves as "a drop of reason in a pool of confusion."[2] An article about the Bible concluded by saying:

> *The greatest obstacle to our peace and survival is the foolish, irrational, delusion that the Bible is "the word of God." If we are to save our children and our world we must accept the fact that the Bible is not the word of God.*[3]

I found the bloated article full of false ideas stated in pompous terms. After reading it, I realized something—Satan is still asking the dangerous question, "Did God really say. . . ?"

Why Believe the Bible Is the Word of God?

I've had times in my life when there was ample opportunity to doubt the goodness of God and the truthfulness of His Word. Yet I have invested my life in teaching and applying that Word of God. I wanted to be certain that the book I base my life upon is trustworthy, so several years ago I began to study various evidences of its reliability and validity. I was stunned to discover that there are so many.

Now, I proudly state that no one who believes in the Bible commits intellectual suicide. I believe there are solid intellectual reasons for believing, reading, and obeying the Bible. I do not believe the Bible *in spite of* the facts, but *because of* the facts.

Entire books have been written on this issue. Allow me to

briefly discuss four compelling reasons for believing the Bible is the trustworthy Word of God.

The Bible Is Indestructible

You would expect that the words of God would have supernatural indestructibility. Isaiah said as much when he wrote, "The grass withers and the flowers fall, but the word of our God stands forever" (Isaiah 40:8). Jesus promised:

> *"I tell you the truth, until heaven and earth disappear, not the smallest letter, not the least stroke of a pen, will by any means disappear from the Law until everything is accomplished."*
>
> MATTHEW 5:18

Throughout history, Satan has used many means and men to attack the Bible. They have all failed.

The Roman emperor Diocletian fiercely attacked the Bible. He killed so many Christians and burned so many Bibles that in AD 303 he erected a pillar inscribed, "The name of Christians has been extinguished."

I don't think so.

Twenty years later, the new Roman emperor, Constantine, saw a vision of the cross and was, amazingly, converted. He not only became a Christian himself, he made Christianity the official religion of Rome. When he asked for a copy of the Bible, the book Diocletian had supposedly wiped out, he was stunned that fifty copies were delivered to him within twenty-four hours. Where had they come from? Each one had been hidden in Diocletian's own palace!

Two hundred years ago, the French atheist Voltaire

declared, "Fifty years from now the world will hear no more of the Bible."

I don't think so.

In fact, fifty years after his death, the Geneva Bible Society bought Voltaire's house and his printing press in order to create even more Bibles. In 1933, the same year a first edition copy of Voltaire's book was selling for eight cents in Paris bookshops, the British Museum bought a copy of the New Testament from Russia for a half million dollars. Two hundred years after Voltaire's death, the Bible exceeded a half billion copies in print![4]

I could tell you one true story after another. Make no mistake about it. The Bible is the indestructible Word of God!

The Bible Is Scientifically Accurate

Some have said they cannot believe the Bible because of apparent contradictions with science. I have come to believe "apparent contradictions with science" are some of the best reasons *for* believing the Bible. Let me explain: The Bible, written over a period of fifteen hundred years by nearly forty different men, is an ancient book that demonstrates astounding scientific accuracy.

Let's look at four facts about science and the Bible:

1. Although it is not a science book, the Bible speaks accurately on scientific subjects. God is truth. Therefore, God cannot lie. The Bible is the Word of God. Therefore, it cannot lie. When it speaks, it speaks truth. When it speaks on scientific matters, it speaks accurately.

2. Because the Bible is an ancient book written thousands of years ago, the authors, although speaking accurately, were

limited to expressing themselves in the language of their day. They do not say God superintends "hydrology: the water cycle," but they explain it.[5]

3. Through the ages, the Bible has contradicted some scientific theories. Yet, as science has developed, science has also contradicted itself! Ninety-nine percent of science books are considered out-of-date in a few years. The world's largest museum, the Louvre in Paris, has three miles of out-of-date science books.[6]

4. Therefore, when science and the Bible contradict, relax. Give science a few hundred years or so, and it will catch up. A scientist named Henry Morris has written:

    One of the most arresting evidences for the inspiration of the Bible is the great number of scientific truths that have lain hidden within its pages for thirty centuries or more, only to be discovered by man's enterprise within the last few centuries or even [the last few] *years.*[7]

Here are a few examples of how the Bible contradicted science until science later caught up:

1. Until AD 1400, science taught that the world was flat. Columbus proved otherwise in 1492. Yet the Bible, in Isaiah 40:22 (written about 700 BC), states that the earth is a circle! Luke 17:30–35, written around AD 60, indicates that people are experiencing both day and night on the earth at the same time. It only took science two thousand years to catch up with what the Bible said in 700 BC!

2. Since its early history, science held that the world was resting on pillars (or even the back of a turtle) until

Sir Isaac Newton discovered the law of gravity in 1687. Yet the Bible, in Job 26:7, described the world as hanging in space. Job was written well over three thousand years ago!

3. In the seventeenth century, Galileo discovered that the winds traveled in circuitous patterns and had weight. Yet, Ecclesiastes 1:6, written in 900 BC, describes the circuits of winds. Job 28:25, written around 1500 BC, tells us that the wind has weight. It only took science three thousand years to catch up with the Bible![8]

The Bible Is a Book of Fulfilled Prophecy

"I am the LORD; that is my name! I will not give my glory to another or my praise to idols. See, the former things have taken place, and new things I declare; before they spring into being I announce them to you."

ISAIAH 42:8–9

God states that His existence can be proved because He tells us what will happen *before* it happens. We know the Bible is the Word of God because it has told us, on hundreds of occasions, what would happen before it happened.

The Bible is the only ancient book with detailed predictive prophecies. If just a few of these prophecies came true, it would be impressive—but you need to understand that *hundreds* of predictive prophecies have come true. Many of these prophecies came true hundreds, and in some cases, thousands of years after they were made! This is an overwhelming reason to believe the Bible.

In the Bible, we have many examples of God predicting the destruction of cities, the rise of leaders and nations, and the details of certain people's lives. We will see in a later chapter, incredible details about the birth, life, death, and resurrection of the Messiah that were predicted in the Bible hundreds of years before those events transpired. In the Bible, God has described the end-times world events in detail. We are starting to see them occur before our very eyes, thousands of years after the prophecies were made.

"He Changed My Life"

These words summarize the story of a skeptic named Josh. As a practical young man, he says he "chucked religion." But God put some real Christians in Josh's life. They had something he knew he lacked, and he was curious. They challenged him to examine the claims of Christ for himself. Yet, Josh was skeptical.

> *I thought it was a farce. In fact, I thought most Christians were walking idiots. . . . I imagined that if a Christian had a brain cell it would die of loneliness.*[9]

But Josh's friends kept challenging him, and eventually he accepted their dare to thoroughly investigate the Bible. He writes:

> *Finally, out of pride, I accepted their challenge. I did it to refute them. I didn't know there were facts. I didn't know that there was evidence that a person could evaluate.*[10]

Josh was determined to win the argument and silence the Christians. He thought it would be easy. He was wrong.

*I set out to refute Christianity. When I couldn't, I
ended up becoming a Christian. I have spent fifteen
years documenting why I believe faith in Jesus Christ is
intellectually feasible.*[11]

Josh McDowell is one of the multitudes who trust the
words of the Bible because it has positively changed their
lives. What other book has had such a powerful effect on so
many people?

Did God Really Say. . . ?

Is the Bible really the Word of God? You'd better believe it. It
is indestructible. It is scientifically accurate. The Bible is full of
detailed predictions that have come true, and it changes lives.
It has changed mine. It will change yours. Trust it, study it,
live it, and share it.

Notes

1. Derek Kidner, *Genesis* (London: Tyndale Press, 1967), p.67.
2. http://www.infidels.org/ (accessed June 20, 2007).
3. "Word of God Debate," Internet Infidels, http://www.infidels.org/library/modern/emmett_fields/word_of_god_debate.html (accessed June 20, 2007).
4. H.L. Wilmington, *The Manuscript From Outer Space* (Lynchburg, VA: self-published textbook, 1974), pp. 92-93.
5. John Macarthur, *Why I Trust the Bible* (Wheaton, IL: Victor Books, 1983), 88.
6. H.L. Wilmington, pp. 110.
7. Henry M. Morris, *The Bible and Modern Science* (Chicago, IL: Moody Press, 1951), p. 7
8. H.L. Wilmington, pp. 100-102.

9. Josh McDowell, *Evidence that Demands a Verdict* (San Bernardino, CA: Here's Life Publishers, 1979) p.16.
10. Ibid.
11. Ibid.

Is There Any God Besides Me?

ISAIAH 44:8

Several years ago, I was out of town taking a doctoral studies course. One evening after a long day of study, I went to the local YMCA where I exercised, showered, then lowered my tired, aching body into a hot tub. Soon, a big, red-haired fellow joined me, and before long, we struck up a conversation. He was a fascinating man, having served around the world in various military and business capacities. He enjoyed talking about himself and fancied himself an authority on many things. I found much of what he said quite interesting.

After a while, as I often do, I attempted to bring Jesus into the conversation. The man had been talkative before, but now became positively enthusiastic in telling me of his religious odyssey. He had studied all of the major religions, he said, and indicated he was an expert in all of them. His journey had led him to conclude that all religions were comparable and that his own brand of New Age religion—with himself as god—was best. In defending this Eastern model of faith, he used an old Indian tale of blind men who tried to describe an elephant. The story goes like this:

Once upon a time, a king gathered a few men who were born blind. They were asked to describe an elephant, but each one was presented with only a certain part of the animal. One man was positioned near the head of the elephant, another near the trunk, one by an ear, another by a leg, one next to the body, another near the tail, and the last by the tuft of the tail.

The man near the head said: "The elephant is like a pot!" The one by the trunk answered, "The elephant is like a hose." The one who touched only the ears thought that the elephant was a fan. The others said that it was a pillar, a wall, a rope, or a brush, depending on the part of the elephant they encountered.

Then they quarreled among themselves, each thinking that he was right and the others wrong. The obvious truth is that the elephant is a unity of many parts, a unity that the men could not grasp in their limited knowledge.

My new friend used this story to show that, when put together, all world religions form a unity. Then, in a very patronizing tone, he informed me that, "Only this unity provides the right perspective on ultimate truth."

I could agree that the elephant tale was indeed a fine story. But I pointed out one fatal flaw in the man's analogy—the God of the Bible is not an elephant!

Is There Any God Besides Me?

Seven hundred years before Jesus, the nation of Judah was, spiritually speaking, like a wife cheating on her husband. In her empty religious ritualism, she played a sham with her husband—the Lord—while at the same time committing spiritual adultery by worshiping idols. The nation hung in the balance of decision.

Was the Lord God of the Bible just another god or was He something more? The Lord Himself posed a dangerous question through His prophet Isaiah.

*"This is what the LORD says—Israel's King and Redeemer, the LORD Almighty: I am the first and I am the last; apart from me there is no God. Who then is like me? Let him proclaim it. Let him declare and lay out before me what has happened since I established my ancient people, and what is yet to come—yes, let him foretell what will come. Do not tremble, do not be afraid. Did I not proclaim this and foretell it long ago? You are my witnesses. **Is there any God besides me?** No, there is no other Rock; I know not one."*

ISAIAH 44:6–8

No Comparison!

Are all gods created equal? Not according to the God of the Bible. Using Isaiah as His messenger, God repeatedly and boldly claimed to be unique and superior, incomparably the only true God—and, therefore, worthy alone of our worship.

"I, even I, am the LORD, and apart from me there is no savior."

ISAIAH 43:11

"I am the LORD, and there is no other; apart from me there is no God. . . . There is none besides me. I am the LORD, and there is no other."

ISAIAH 45:5–6

"There is no God apart from me, a righteous God and a Savior; there is none but me. Turn to me and be saved, all you ends of the earth; for I am God, and there is no other."

ISAIAH 45:21–22

"To whom will you compare me or count me equal? To whom will you liken me that we may be compared?"

ISAIAH 46:5

"I am God, and there is no other; I am God, and there is none like me."

ISAIAH 46:9

What basis does God have for such bold assertions? In Isaiah, He verifies His claims based on His unique ability to forecast the future.

The God of the Bible Accurately Predicts the Future

When God spoke through His prophet Isaiah, He revealed His displeasure with the defection of many Israelites from the true worship of Himself to the worthless worship of manmade gods and nature deities. God argued that He had the right to demand their worship because He was able to accurately tell the future. He challenged the people's false gods to do the same.

"Present your case," says the LORD. "Set forth your arguments," says Jacob's King. "Bring in your idols to tell us what is going to happen. Tell us what the former things were, so that we may consider them and know their final outcome. Or declare to us the things to come, tell us what the future holds, so we may know that you are gods. Do something, whether good or bad, so that we will be dismayed and filled with fear."

ISAIAH 41:21-23

Accurately predicting the future presumes at least one of two abilities: 1) the power to cause history to unfold in a certain way, and 2) the power to step outside of the constraints of time.[1] The God of the Bible could do both. Read what He said:

> *"This is what the LORD says—Israel's King and Redeemer, the LORD Almighty: I am the first and I am the last; apart from me there is no God. Who then is like me? Let him proclaim it. Let him declare and lay out before me what has happened since I established my ancient people, and what is yet to come—yes, let him foretell what will come. Do not tremble, do not be afraid. Did I not proclaim this and foretell it long ago? You are my witnesses. Is there any God besides me? No, there is no other Rock; I know not one."*
>
> ISAIAH 44:6–8

> *"Remember the former things, those of long ago; I am God, and there is no other; I am God, and there is none like me. I make known the end from the beginning, from ancient times, what is still to come. I say: My purpose will stand, and I will do all that I please."*
>
> ISAIAH 46:9–10

> *"Gather together and come; assemble, you fugitives from the nations. Ignorant are those who carry about idols of wood, who pray to gods that cannot save. Declare what is to be, present it—let them take counsel together. Who foretold this long ago, who declared it from the distant past? Was it not I, the LORD? And there is no God apart from me, a righteous God and a Savior; there is none but me. Turn to me and be saved, all you ends of the earth; for I am God, and there is no other."*
>
> ISAIAH 45:20–22

> *"I foretold the former things long ago, my mouth announced them and I made them known; then suddenly I acted, and*

*they came to pass. For I knew how stubborn you were; the
sinews of your neck were iron, your forehead was bronze.
Therefore I told you these things long ago; before they
happened I announced them to you so that you could
not say, 'My idols did them; my wooden image and metal
god ordained them.' You have heard these things; look at
them all. Will you not admit them? From now on I will
tell you of new things, of hidden things unknown to you.
They are created now, and not long ago; you have not
heard of them before today. So you cannot say, 'Yes, I knew
of them.' "*

ISAIAH 48:3–7

God showed boldness, even audacity, in predicting the
future, but also wisdom in having each prediction carefully
recorded, accurately copied, and widely distributed *prior to* the
happening of the event. This record is found in the Bible, a book
unlike other religious literature, as it contains the written record
of the prophetic messages of God, some recorded hundreds of
years in advance of the happenings. Each is fulfilled in minute
detail and proves that He indeed is the only true God.

It is beyond the scope of this book to detail all the amazing
predictions God made and their detailed fulfillment. But allow
me to mention a few of my favorite examples.

Cyrus

Around 700 BC, Isaiah recorded God's prediction that a man
named Cyrus would rebuild the temple of Jerusalem (Isaiah
44:28, 45:13). At the time the prediction was made, the
temple in Jerusalem had not been destroyed. But, sure enough,
about 120 years later the city and temple were destroyed by
the Babylonian king, Nebuchadnezzar. Shortly after that, the

Babylonians were conquered by the Persians. Several years later, 160 years after the prophecy of Isaiah, a Persian king, who happened to be named *Cyrus*, gave the order to rebuild the temple (Ezra 1:1–4)!

Tyre and Sidon

The prophet Ezekiel recorded a stunningly detailed prophecy of judgment against the powerful ancient city of Tyre (Ezekiel 26). God specifically said: 1) Nebuchadnezzar would destroy the mainland of Tyre; 2) many nations would come against it; 3) she would be flattened like a table rock; 4) fisherman would spread their nets over the place the city once stood; 5) the debris of the city would be thrown into the water; 6) she would never be rebuilt; and 7) she would never be found again. Over the course of hundreds of years, each of these seven events has occurred. Mathematician Peter Stoner evaluated the miracle with this conclusion.

> *If Ezekiel had looked at Tyre in his day and had made these seven predictions in human wisdom, these estimates mean that there would have been only one chance in 75,000,000 of coming true. These all came true in the minutest detail.*[2]

Ezekiel also records a prediction regarding Tyre's sister city, Sidon (Ezekiel 28). Unlike Tyre, she would not be destroyed but would suffer a relentless series of bloody conquests and battles. Exactly as predicted, Sidon has suffered ongoing bloodshed, having been captured again and again, especially during the Crusades. Yet the city of Sidon is still standing today.

The Jewish People

Four thousand years ago, God predicted that a man named Abram would father a great nation, become a blessing to all nations, and have a land that would forever belong to his descendents (Genesis 12:2–3, 13:14–16). Seven hundred years later, a nation of millions arose and moved into their own land (Joshua 1 and following). When they disobeyed God, He allowed them to be taken captive and carried away from their land. They returned for a short time, but were expelled again by the Romans in AD 70.

Seemingly, God's promise had failed. The Jewish people wandered the earth experiencing persecution on every side—culminating in Adolf Hitler's Holocaust of World War II, when six million European Jews were murdered. Amazingly, though, unlike other people groups throughout history, Abram's nation never lost its corporate identity. Against all odds, after 1,878 years in exile, on May 14, 1948, the nation-state of Israel was reborn!

Jesus

As I've already mentioned, Jesus didn't fulfill only one or two Bible prophecies. Instead, there are upwards of 332 distinct predictions fulfilled by the lineage, birth, life, death, and resurrection of Jesus Christ![3] Incredible details about Him were written hundreds of years before they occurred. Through David (Psalm 22) and Isaiah (Isaiah 53), God describes details of the Messiah's death on the cross, an instrument of execution not even invented until years after the prophecies were recorded!

Doubt Quencher

Is there any God besides the Lord God of the Bible? Should we ever wonder if He is the only true God?

When doubts arise in my mind, I quickly quench them by reminding myself of the hundreds of distinct, detailed predictions about future events that God has literally fulfilled. The odds of such "coincidences" make doubt an absolute impossibility. The God of the Bible is unique, incomparable, and superior to all others. Worship Him!

Place God where He belongs in your life. Elevate Him above all else that clamors to be God of your life. Exalt Him above every hobby, job, career, possession, title, position, ministry, and relationship. Put Him ahead of yourself.

He alone is God. There is no other!

Notes

1. Dennis McCallum, *Christianity, the Faith that Makes Sense* (Wheaton, IL: Tyndale House, 1992), 61.
2. Peter Stoner, *Science Speaks* (Chicago: Moody Press, 1963), 80.
3. Floyd Hamilton, *The Basis of Christian Faith* (New York: Harper and Row, 1964), 160.

Is There Not a Cause?

1 SAMUEL 17:29 KJV

It was the worst of times. The Philistines had brought all their ferocious armies together to attack Judah. King Saul and the men of Israel faced them on the other side of the valley of Elah. The Philistines sent out their champion, Goliath the giant, to challenge Israel's strongest man to a winner-take-all, man-to-man rumble.

But Israel had no champion—at least none willing to fight the Philistine monster. Standing over nine feet tall, strong enough to wear a 125-pound coat of mail, one look at Goliath made the men of Israel, including King Saul, shrink back in fear (1 Samuel 17:1–11). After forty days of Goliath's twice-daily challenges and taunts, the entire Israelite army cowered in despair.

But one Israelite saw the battle from a different perspective. A teenager named David had left his flock to attend to three older brothers who were members of the army (1 Samuel 17:12–22). When David saw the arrogant Goliath, something snapped inside him. A holy passion erupted from deep within. He turned to the soldiers around him and asked:

> *"What will be done for the man who kills this Philistine and removes this disgrace from Israel? Who is this uncircumcised Philistine that he should defy the armies of the living God?"*
>
> 1 SAMUEL 17:26

The teen's bravado did not play well in the Israelite camp, especially within David's own family. When his brother, Eliab, heard David's response, he mocked and belittled his young sibling. But David saw the battle from God's perspective—and his outlook would ultimately determine its outcome. David's godly ardor was aroused, and he was unable to resist blurting out a very dangerous question.

> *What have I now done?* **Is there not a cause?**
>
> 1 SAMUEL 17:29 KJV

"Is There Not a Cause?"

David saw what no one else did: the big picture, the divine point of view. He realized that this battle was not merely between two men, or even two armies. When Goliath taunted the Israelites, he was mocking God—and David saw that someone needed to stand for the Lord's cause!

Surely, he knew that he alone, a scrawny youth, would be no match for a giant warrior, a veteran soldier and experienced killer. But David's hope wasn't in himself. God had gone with him before, and God could be counted on to go with him again. When questioned, he explained to Israel's King Saul:

> *"Your servant has been keeping his father's sheep. When a lion or a bear came and carried off a sheep from the flock, I went after it, struck it and rescued the sheep from its mouth. When it turned on me, I seized it by its hair, struck it and killed it. Your servant has killed both the lion and the bear; this uncircumcised Philistine will be like one of them, because he has defied the armies of the living God. The LORD who delivered me from the paw of the lion*

*and the paw of the bear will deliver me from the hand of
this Philistine."*

1 SAMUEL 17:34–37

"The Lord who delivered me. . .will deliver me." David's
bold self-confidence was rooted in a deep God-reliance. The
Lord was David's hope—and only hope—for victory. Would
the Lord be enough? Let's see.

The Battle Is the Lord's

David refused Saul's unfamiliar armor and instead entered
combat with the staff and slingshot he had successfully
used as a shepherd. When he approached Goliath, the giant
warrior scorned him for his puny size, tender age, and general
inexperience. Goliath "cursed David by his gods" (1 Samuel
17:43) and mocked him by saying, "Come here. . .and I'll give
your flesh to the birds of the air and the beasts of the field!"
(17:44).

At this point, most intelligent men would have turned
and run as fast as they could—but not David, because he was
directed by the cause of God. Goliath had crossed the line.
He had gone too far. He was going down because David was
fighting for the name of the Lord.

*David said to the Philistine, "You come against me with
sword and spear and javelin, but I come against you in
the name of the LORD Almighty, the God of the armies
of Israel, whom you have defied. This day the LORD will
hand you over to me, and I'll strike you down and cut off
your head. Today I will give the carcasses of the Philistine
army to the birds of the air and the beasts of the earth,
and the whole world will know that there is a God in*

> *Israel. All those gathered here will know that it is not by*
> *sword or spear that the LORD saves; for the battle is the*
> *LORD's, and he will give all of you into our hands."*
> 1 SAMUEL 17:45–47

I love David's courageous confidence. He believed that
the Lord is bigger than any giant—especially this pagan
blasphemer—and that it would be no contest. David was
certain that God could wipe out this enemy without his help.
He understood that he was merely the tool God was using to
bring about Goliath's and the Philistines' defeat. So instead of
running away, he ran *toward* Goliath in full attack mode.

> *As the Philistine moved closer to attack him, David ran*
> *quickly toward the battle line to meet him. Reaching into*
> *his bag and taking out a stone, he slung it and struck*
> *the Philistine on the forehead. The stone sank into his*
> *forehead, and he fell facedown on the ground.*
>
> *So David triumphed over the Philistine with a sling*
> *and a stone; without a sword in his hand he struck down*
> *the Philistine and killed him.*
>
> *David ran and stood over him. He took hold of the*
> *Philistine's sword and drew it from the scabbard. After he*
> *killed him, he cut off his head with the sword.*
> 1 SAMUEL 17:48–51

That didn't take long! One God-directed stone from a
slingshot and the enemy was down—and quickly decapitated.
One boy plus God proved to be a clear majority, an army that
was more than Goliath could handle.

But Goliath wasn't the only loser that day.

> *When the Philistines saw that their hero was dead, they*
> *turned and ran. Then the men of Israel and Judah surged*

*forward with a shout and pursued the Philistines to the
entrance of Gath and to the gates of Ekron. Their dead
were strewn along the Shaaraim road to Gath and Ekron.
When the Israelites returned from chasing the Philistines,
they plundered their camp.*

1 SAMUEL 17:51–53

David changed history because he lived for a cause larger
than himself. He wasn't the only one. Many have changed the
world when they answered the question, "Is there not a cause?"

Wilberforce's Cause

William Wilberforce was elected to parliament as a twenty-
one-year-old student in 1780. A few years later, he experienced
what he later called the "Great Change" as Christ became the
center of his life. Wilberforce briefly considered abandoning
Parliament to enter the clergy, but supporters persuaded him
that he could serve God more effectively in public life. He
knew that his new commitment might cost him friends and
influence, but he was determined to act on what he now
believed.

Wilberforce said that God gave him two great causes,
including the "renewal of society." He led an attack on vices
such as drinking and gambling that afflicted and demoralized
the poor. He called on the upper classes to introduce true
Christian values into their lives. He contributed to a Sunday
school program that provided children with regular education
in reading, personal hygiene, and religion.

His second great cause was the primary area of his
activism: a lifelong, lonely, and unpopular battle to abolish
slavery in England. Nearly fifty years of uphill effort paid off
when, three days before his death in 1833, Wilberforce heard

that the House of Commons had passed a law emancipating all slaves in Britain's colonies. A major motion picture in 2007, *Amazing Grace*, commemorated his courageous battle against human bondage.

Find Your Cause and Go for It

Ordinary people can make an extraordinary difference if they sell out to God's cause. David fought a giant and saved a nation. William Wilberforce abolished slavery in England, starting a process that ended the practice in the United States, too. I challenge you to ask yourself:

What has God uniquely gifted, trained, and prepared me to do?

What need breaks my heart?

What sight makes my blood boil?

What cause will I spend the rest of my life for?

What would I die for?

13

Who Knows but That You Have Come. . . for Such a Time as This?

ESTHER 4:14

Have you ever wondered why you are where you are right now? Are you in a particular job or ministry or personal relationship by accident? Is your life merely the result of random decisions and consequences?

I doubt it. That certainly wasn't the case for a girl named Esther.

Bad News for the Jews

Nearly twenty-five hundred years ago in the land of Persia, a high government official had way too much power. Haman, the king's second in command, hoped to use his status to elevate himself and eradicate God's people, the Jews.

One day, Haman's boss, King Xerxes, ordered all his servants to show honor to Haman by bowing before him. But one man refused—the good and godly Jew, Mordecai. He would only bow before the true God, and Haman simply didn't qualify.

When Haman discovered Mordecai's attitude, he was incensed and hatched a sinister plot: He would get back at Mordecai by annihilating every Jew in the kingdom. Haman obtained Xerxes' approval for his plan by dishonestly telling the king of a people "whose customs are different from those of all other people and who do not obey the king's laws" (Esther 3:8). Haman even offered to pay for the program, figuring the plunder of all the Jews in the vast Persian kingdom would generate the millions of dollars it would take to kill them.

All looked grim for the Jews. But there is more to this story.

The Dangerous Question

"Coincidentally," not long before, the king had become disillusioned with his wife and sought out a new one. A nationwide beauty contest was held to find a new queen for Xerxes. A beautiful girl named Esther caught the king's eye and won the tiara. Xerxes fell deeply in love with Esther and made her queen of the realm. "It just so happened" that Esther was Jewish—and Mordecai was her cousin.

When Mordecai learned that Haman was planning to wipe out the Jews, he told Esther's bodyguard of the terrible tragedy awaiting their people. But Esther felt powerless to help. In Persia, at that time, a queen couldn't approach a king uninvited. To do so could incur the death penalty. But at that point, Mordecai asked Esther a most dangerous question.

> *"Do not think that because you are in the king's house you alone of all the Jews will escape. For if you remain silent at this time, relief and deliverance for the Jews will arise from another place, but you and your father's family will perish. And **who knows but that you have come** to royal position **for such a time as this?**"*
>
> ESTHER 4:13–14

"For Such a Time as This?"

This question put Esther between the proverbial rock and a hard place. No matter how she responded, she could die. To act would surely risk her life with the king. To fail to act would be to condemn all Jews—including herself—to certain death.

But Mordecai was wise in his approach and choice of words. "Look," he basically said, "Here you are—a Jewish girl—in the king's palace, living large as the favored wife of the most powerful man on earth. You have no business being there apart from the sovereign workings of God. Surely, He's put you here for a higher purpose." In Esther's unique position, she was one of very few people with intimate access to the king. Her people needed her. No one else could help. She was their only hope.

"If I Perish, I Perish"

What did Esther do? Play it safe and avoid the issue? Or take a risk and get involved? She didn't waste much time pondering her options:

> Then Esther sent this reply to Mordecai: "Go, gather together all the Jews who are in Susa, and fast for me. Do not eat or drink for three days, night or day. I and my maids will fast as you do. When this is done, I will go to the king, even though it is against the law. And if I perish, I perish."
>
> ESTHER 4:15–16

I love Esther's fearlessness as she put it all on the line. I agree with Erwin McManus who wrote,

*I am convinced that the great tragedy is not the sins that
we commit, but the life that we fail to live. You cannot
follow God in neutral. God created you to do something.*[1]

Henry Blackaby writes, "You cannot continue life as usual
or stay where you are, and go with God at the same time."[2] It's
true throughout scripture—God calls us to take risks.

Noah could not continue life as usual and build an ark at
the same time—he had to risk looking foolish. Moses could
not stay in the desert herding sheep and fearlessly stand before
Pharaoh at the same time—he had to risk facing his past.

Joshua took a risk when he followed God's command to
step into the Jordan River, believing it would open to allow his
army to cross it. He took a risk marching around the walls of
Jericho seven times.

Ruth risked the familiar to strike out with her mother-
in-law. Gideon took a risk to face an army of thousands with
only three hundred men. David embraced a huge risk by
facing Goliath with only a slingshot. Elijah took a risk when he
challenged a wicked king and queen and 850 false prophets to
a spiritual duel.

Peter, Andrew, James, and John left the security of their
fishing business to follow Jesus. Matthew left his lucrative tax
booth to become Jesus' disciple. Paul risked his life repeatedly
to take the gospel to the Gentiles.

Esther Took the Risk

The people fasted as the queen had requested. Then Esther,
buoyed by the knowledge that she was not queen by accident,
bravely approached Xerxes. When Esther came before the king,
he didn't order her execution. Instead, he was so pleased to
see her he blurted, "What is your request? Even up to half the

kingdom, it will be given you" (Esther 5:3).

Esther waited to answer, patiently asking her husband to come the next night, along with Haman, for a banquet. Twenty-four hours later, the king enjoyed a special meal and offered once again to give Esther anything she desired, up to half his kingdom. But again she delayed, knowing the king wasn't yet ready to grant her huge request. Esther simply invited Xerxes and Haman back the next night for another feast.

Viewing the two royal dinner invitations as good fortune, Haman figured he could now do whatever he wanted. So he ordered the construction of a monstrous, seventy-five-foot tall gallows. He planned to ask the king the next day to order the execution of Mordecai.

God Was at Work Behind the Scenes

That evening, the king was strangely restless. He couldn't fall asleep, so he ordered a record of the daily events of his reign read to him. An interesting item was mentioned, one that the king had somehow forgotten or perhaps never heard about. Some time earlier, Mordecai had uncovered a plot to assassinate the king. His good citizenship spared the king's life. But Mordecai had inadvertently gone unrewarded.

Early the next morning, Haman arrived at the king's chamber to ask permission to execute his nemesis, Mordecai. But before he could make his request, Xerxes asked Haman what could be done to honor someone special to the king. Blinded by his own arrogance, Haman assumed the king was talking about him—and Haman poured out a lavish plan involving a royal robe, the king's horse, and an official court crier to shout, "This is what is done for the man the king delights to honor!" (Esther 6:9).

The king loved the idea and ordered Haman to carry it out—for Mordecai!

Later that night, the king and Haman dined at Esther's table. Again, Xerxes gushed that he'd gladly give Esther up to half of his kingdom. Now was the time. God had brought Esther to the palace for such a time as this. So she said,

> *"If I have found favor with you, O king, and if it pleases your majesty, grant me my life—this is my petition. And spare my people—this is my request."*
>
> ESTHER 7:3

I imagine Esther gulping after making her request. But the king had no anger toward her—he was livid against her adversary, demanding to know the villain's name. To Haman's horror, she boldly pointed him out and said, "The adversary and enemy is this vile Haman" (Esther 7:6).

In fury, the king stomped out of the room.

Then Haman made his final mistake. Groveling at the couch where Esther reclined, begging for his life, he got a little too close to the queen. When Xerxes returned, he saw Haman hovering awkwardly over Esther and asked incredulously, "Will he even molest the queen while she is with me in the house?" (Esther 7:8).

> *Then Harbona, one of the eunuchs attending the king, said, "A gallows seventy-five feet high stands by Haman's house. He had it made for Mordecai, who spoke up to help the king."*
>
> *The king said, "Hang him on it!" So they hanged Haman on the gallows he had prepared for Mordecai. Then the king's fury subsided.*
>
> ESTHER 7:9–10

Add It Up

Esther answered her dangerous question appropriately. As a result, though things looked dicey for a while, the good guys staged a rally and crushed the villains. God won a great victory. Add up the score:

1. Bad guy Haman threatens to kill all Jews, starting with Mordecai. Good Guys 0, Bad Guys 1.
2. But instead of killing all the Jews, Haman is forced to honor Mordecai. Good Guys 1, Bad Guys 1.
3. Haman is hanged on the gallows he built to kill Mordecai. But that's not all—the rest of the story would have been considered absolutely impossible just a few days earlier. Good Guys 2, Bad Guys 1.
4. Instead of the death penalty for approaching the king, Esther receives her own palace—Haman's former estate! Good Guys 3, Bad Guys 1.
5. Esther is given the power to spare all the Jews. Good Guys 4, Bad Guys 1.
6. Beyond that, the Jews are given authority to kill those who had persecuted them and to confiscate their property. Good Guys 5, Bad Guys 1.
7. As a result, many non-Jews decide to become Jews! Good Guys 6, Bad Guys 1.
8. If that's not enough, Mordecai, instead of being the first Jew killed, is honored as a hero *and* is given Haman's position as the king's highest-ranking official. Good Guys 7, Bad Guys 1!

All of these victories came after Esther faced a dangerous question and risked giving the right answer.

I wonder: Are you currently facing a tough situation or decision? Why does God have you in the position you're in?

Will you trust that He hasn't made a mistake? Will you take a risk in order to really follow Him?

Notes

1. Erwin McManus, *Seizing Your Divine Moment* (Nashville: Thomas Nelson, Inc., 2002), 34–35.
2. Henry Blackaby, *Experiencing God* (Nashville: Broadman & Holman Publishers, 1994), 234.

14

Does Job Fear God for Nothing?

JOB 1:9

Why do you worship God? Out of fear or love or gratitude? To receive blessings from the Lord? To impress others? Is guilt your motivation?

Do you love God only when blessings flow? Do you draw back from God when things don't go your way? Does your situation determine your motivation for serving Him?

These are dangerous questions indeed.

Why Do You Worship the Lord?

One day long ago, Satan asked a question that profoundly affected the life of one man, his family, his employees, and probably his entire community. The question still has the power to dynamically change lives today.

The Scene

In the land of Uz there lived a man whose name was Job. This man was blameless and upright; he feared God and shunned evil. He had seven sons and three daughters, and he owned seven thousand sheep, three thousand camels,

*five hundred yoke of oxen and five hundred donkeys, and
had a large number of servants. He was the greatest man
among all the people of the East.*

JOB 1:1–3

The opening scene seems harmless enough. A good
man named Job is blessed with a great family and a
prosperous business. But behind the scenes, something
sinister lurks.

The Unseen Scene

As you may know, God and Satan are locked in a cosmic battle
for loyalty and allegiance. Sometimes *we* are the battleground.
Job couldn't hear the dangerous question that would suddenly
change his entire life.

> *Then the LORD said to Satan, "Have you considered
> my servant Job? There is no one on earth like him; he
> is blameless and upright, a man who fears God and
> shuns evil."*
> **"Does Job fear God for nothing?"** *Satan replied.
> "Have you not put a hedge around him and his household
> and everything he has? You have blessed the work of his
> hands, so that his flocks and herds are spread throughout
> the land. But stretch out your hand and strike everything
> he has, and he will surely curse you to your face."*
> *The LORD said to Satan, "Very well, then, everything
> he has is in your hands, but on the man himself do not lay
> a finger."*
> *Then Satan went out from the presence of the LORD.*

JOB 1:8–12

Notice carefully Satan's question. It is one of the most dangerous ever uttered: "Does Job fear God for nothing?"

In other words, "Will a man continue to loyally follow God even when he is overwhelmed by unexpected, unprovoked, inexplicable evil? Is God really worth it? Does He merit such loyalty?"

Satan knew that *he* didn't merit loyalty in spite of adversity. No one would follow him unless he bribed them. He simply isn't worth it. But blinded by his own arrogance and jealousy, Satan refused to believe that God is worth such allegiance. So, based on one dangerous question, he proposed a high-stakes chess game with poor Job serving as a pawn.

Surprisingly, God played along.

Disaster Strikes

Satan wasted no time in ambushing Job. He struck and struck quickly, thoroughly, and very, very hard.

> *One day when Job's sons and daughters were feasting and drinking wine at the oldest brother's house, a messenger came to Job and said, "The oxen were plowing and the donkeys were grazing nearby, and the Sabeans attacked and carried them off. They put the servants to the sword, and I am the only one who has escaped to tell you!"*
>
> *While he was still speaking, another messenger came and said, "The fire of God fell from the sky and burned up the sheep and the servants, and I am the only one who has escaped to tell you!"*
>
> *While he was still speaking, another messenger came and said, "The Chaldeans formed three raiding parties and swept down on your camels and carried them off. They put the servants to the sword, and I am the only*

one who has escaped to tell you!"

While he was still speaking, yet another messenger
came and said, "Your sons and daughters were feasting
and drinking wine at the oldest brother's house, when
suddenly a mighty wind swept in from the desert and
struck the four corners of the house. It collapsed on them
and they are dead, and I am the only one who has escaped
to tell you!"

JOB 1:13–19

"Does Job Fear God for Nothing?"

This is a very dangerous question on several levels. First, because
it led to devastating tragedy, it was dangerous for Job. He lost
his children, his employees, his property, and his reputation.
Second, it was potentially dangerous for God. If Job turned his
back, it would be an affront to the Lord's intrinsic worth. Third,
it was risky for the devil. If Job remained true to God, it would
be a major victory for the Lord.

How did Job answer the question? Did he truly believe
God was worthy of worship even when everything was taken
away?

After the last terrible report that his children had all been
killed by a tornado, Job gave his answer.

At this, Job got up and tore his robe and shaved his head.
Then he fell to the ground in worship and said: "Naked
I came from my mother's womb, and naked I will depart.
The LORD gave and the LORD has taken away; may the
name of the LORD be praised."

In all this, Job did not sin by charging God with
wrongdoing.

JOB 1:20–22

What an answer! Crushed, broken, aching, and numb, Job refused to turn on God. He even used his grief over his loss as an opportunity for worship.

Did Job fear God for nothing? His answer was loud and clear. "No!" Job feared God for *something*—the intrinsic worth of God demands worship no matter what!

Suddenly, the cosmic question became very dangerous for Satan. The devil had hoped to bring God's worth into question. But Job's response was so heroically clear that, instead, the amazing worth of God's character was reaffirmed.

The Unseen Scene, Part 2

Satan didn't quit. His stubborn resiliency and persistence are impressive, so he moved on to plan B.

> *Then the* LORD *said to Satan, "Have you considered my servant Job? There is no one on earth like him; he is blameless and upright, a man who fears God and shuns evil. And he still maintains his integrity, though you incited me against him to ruin him without any reason."*
>
> *"Skin for skin!" Satan replied. "A man will give all he has for his own life. But stretch out your hand and strike his flesh and bones, and he will surely curse you to your face."*
>
> JOB 2:3–5

Again, Satan questioned God's integrity by attacking Job's. He asked permission to attack the suffering man's health. God agreed and Job got blindsided. . .again.

> *The* LORD *said to Satan, "Very well, then, he is in your hands; but you must spare his life."*

So Satan went out from the presence of the LORD and afflicted Job with painful sores from the soles of his feet to the top of his head. Then Job took a piece of broken pottery and scraped himself with it as he sat among the ashes.

JOB 2:6–8

I have had boils. They're brutal. They are ugly, swollen, angry red sores that have to be lanced to bring even the slightest relief. One boil is sheer misery. Being covered from head to toe with them would be off-the-charts, relentless agony. If his emotional grief wasn't bad enough, Job now had to endure severe physical suffering. No wonder his already grief-stricken wife gave him such sour advice.

His wife said to him, "Are you still holding on to your integrity? Curse God and die!"

JOB 2:9

"Does Job Fear God for Nothing?" Part 2

He replied, "You are talking like a foolish woman. Shall we accept good from God, and not trouble?"
In all this, Job did not sin in what he said.

JOB 2:10

Agony piled upon agony, torment heaped upon torment, sorrow loaded upon sorrow—yet Job remained loyal to the Lord. He refused to turn on God. In spite of the severity of his suffering, Job worshiped God.

Satan's great gamble blew up in his face.

God's risk proved worth it.

Job answered the dangerous question heroically.

121

Satan was shamed and silenced. Nowhere is he mentioned in the final forty chapters of the book of Job!

Do You Fear God for Nothing?

I wonder, what would have happened if you'd been in Job's situation? Or me? How would we have responded to such extreme loss? Would you have worshiped Him no matter what? What would it take for you or me to turn our backs on God?

The suffering we face in life might have nothing to do with us but everything to do with God's plan to silence Satan's pride, to shut his boastful mouth. Maybe a dangerous question, with us as the subject, has been asked. Perhaps two entire kingdoms—of darkness and of God—are watching to see how we handle our pain. Will our lives prove that God is truly worthy?[1]

Notes

1. For a practical, encouraging, and detailed study of the question of suffering and evil, see Dave Earley, *The 21 Reasons Bad Things Happen to Good People* (Uhrichsville, OH: Barbour Publishing, 2007).

Have You Any Right to Be Angry?

Jonah 4:4

What is your biggest obstacle?

On two separate occasions, five years apart, I asked the members of my church about the areas where they faced the greatest struggles. The overwhelming response in both surveys was the same: That thing we all struggled with, as growing followers of Jesus, was anger.

Anger is part of human nature. Most flows out of perceived injustice. It's born from the feeling that you're being mistreated—or that someone you care about is being wronged.

It's easy to sin in our anger, but it's also possible to be angry without sin. That's up to us, since anger as an emotion is neutral. What causes our anger and how we handle it is what determines its sinfulness.

As I reviewed every example of anger in the Bible, I was surprised to find so many. There were at least four times as many examples of destructive anger than constructive. I think that's pretty accurate in my own life: I find myself angry over the wrong things, in the wrong way, for the wrong reasons much more often than I feel anger over the right things, in the right way, for the right reasons. Are you like that?

Jealousy may cause our anger (read about Cain in Genesis 4, and Saul in 1 Samuel 18). It could be the self-centered desire to be in control (read about Balak in Numbers 22–24). But the inappropriate cause of anger I wrestle with most often is a desire to claim "my rights." I struggle with a disproportionate sense of entitlement. I get mad when I feel like someone or something is infringing on my right to be listened to, respected, understood, appreciated, recognized, and rewarded the way I want. If you are an entitlement, rights-centered person, you are an angry person.

More than two thousand years ago, one of God's leading men had an anger problem. God asked him a dangerous question that can serve as the key to overcoming inappropriate anger.

Jonah Goes to Nineveh

You probably know the story of Jonah, the wayward prophet. God basically told him, "I want you to go to Nineveh and tell the people there they've got forty days to repent." Nineveh was a wicked, brutal, pagan city. Yet God loved its people and graciously gave them a chance to turn from their sin before judgment fell. Jonah, however, didn't care about Nineveh. He wanted to preach where he wanted to preach. He wanted to preach to the people he wanted to preach to. So he boarded a boat going the opposite direction.

God's response to Jonah's disobedience was, "Hold on, now." The Lord caused a devastating storm to rock Jonah's ship, with wind and waves so severe they frightened the professional sailors on board. To spare his fellow travelers, Jonah came clean, admitting that he was the cause of the storm. At his request, the sailors eventually threw Jonah overboard.

Even now, God was gracious—and provided a big fish to swallow Jonah (Jonah 1:17). If that doesn't sound very gracious, consider this: Jonah was kept alive inside the fish and had time to repent of his selfish rebellion (Jonah 2). You probably would, too, at that point.

Three days later, the fish spits Jonah out, and God restates His command: "Go to the great city of Nineveh and proclaim to it the message I give you" (3:2). This time, Jonah obeys— perhaps grudgingly, but he does what he's told—preaching a message of repentance. And, wonder of wonders, the Ninevites take his message to heart (Jonah 3).

You probably already knew that much of the story. What you might not know is the rest of the story.

Blinded by His Rights

Jonah's message to Nineveh was one of the most influential sermons ever preached. In a city where the people were likely to ignore or even kill Jonah, the miraculous happened. Over one hundred thousand people repented. A large and powerful city was spared judgment. Shouldn't Jonah be dancing for joy?

> *But Jonah was greatly displeased and became angry. He prayed to the LORD, "O LORD, is this not what I said when I was still at home? That is why I was so quick to flee to Tarshish. I knew that you are a gracious and compassionate God, slow to anger and abounding in love, a God who relents from sending calamity. Now, O LORD, take away my life, for it is better for me to die than to live."*
>
> JONAH 4:1–3

Jonah felt he had a right *not* to go to Nineveh. He felt he had the right to preach judgment—and to see judgment fall. All he could see were his rights, and he wanted things to go his way. Jonah completely missed the awesome work of God he had just witnessed. Blinded by his "rights," Jonah held them so tightly that when he didn't get what he wanted, he fell into a suicidal depression.

The Dangerous Question

Cutting through the dark fog of selfish entitlement, God asked a dangerous question.

> But the LORD replied, **"Have you any right to be angry?"**
> JONAH 4:4

One little question—seven simple words—and the key to unlocking a cause and cure of our selfish anger is revealed. *Have you any right to be angry?* This question has the power to expose our hearts, diagnose our anger, and put us on the road to freedom. But before we delve further into that, let's see how Jonah responded.

Silenced by Self-Pity

What did Jonah do when God asked him this question? Nothing. Jonah was so immersed in self-pity that he didn't even reply. He just wandered off in the vague hope that maybe those pagans from Nineveh weren't sincere, and that God would end up zapping them anyway.

> *Jonah went out and sat down at a place east of the city. There he made himself a shelter, sat in its shade and waited to see what would happen to the city. Then the LORD God provided a vine and made it grow up over Jonah to give shade for his head to ease his discomfort, and Jonah was very happy about the vine.*
>
> JONAH 4:5–6

God loved Jonah and blessed him by sending a cooling plant to cheer him. But Jonah sat in the shade, still full of self-pity. He enjoyed his new plant perhaps too much. His heart was still selfish.

God loved Jonah too much to allow him to stay in his self-pitying funk. So God moved on to plan B.

> *But at dawn the next day God provided a worm, which chewed the vine so that it withered. When the sun rose, God provided a scorching east wind, and the sun blazed on Jonah's head so that he grew faint. He wanted to die, and said, "It would be better for me to die than to live."*
>
> JONAH 4:7–8

Some people just don't get it. God was up to big, beautiful things in the lives of people, but Jonah was so selfish he was oblivious to them. All he could see were his rights, his comfort, and his plant.

The Dangerous Question, Part 2

Once again, God cut through Jonah's gloom by asking a similar question.

> *But God said to Jonah, "Do you have a right to be angry about the vine?"*
>
> JONAH 4:9

At this point, we would hope Jonah would drop to his knees and say something like this:

> *"Lord, I am so sorry. Please forgive me for my selfish grasping at rights. Thank You for calling me to come here. Thank You for giving me a second chance when I ran the first time. Thanks for sending the storm to get*

my attention. *Thank You for sending the big fish to save my life. Thank You for letting me preach to these people. Thank You that they listened and repented. Thanks for sending the plant for even a little while.*

"*I don't deserve any of these blessings. I deserve death and hell. I should be the one you destroy.*"

But sadly, Jonah still didn't get it. Read his response to God's question:

> *But God said to Jonah, "Do you have a right to be angry about the vine?"*
> *"I do," he said. "I am angry enough to die."*
>
> JONAH 4:9

Poor Jonah, I say with some sarcasm. All he could see were the violations of his supposed rights. In his eyes, God had sent him where he did not want to go. The Lord had given him a message he did not want to deliver. The people had responded in a way he had hoped they wouldn't. God had given mercy to people whom Jonah did not think deserved it. Then the Lord took his vine. In Jonah's mind, he had every right to be angry—so angry he wanted to die.

The Bigger Picture

> *But the LORD said, "You have been concerned about this vine, though you did not tend it or make it grow. It sprang up overnight and died overnight. But Nineveh has more than a hundred and twenty thousand people who cannot tell their right hand from their left, and many cattle as well. Should I not be concerned about that great city?"*
>
> JONAH 4:10–11

God wanted Jonah to see the bigger picture. If the conversation is about rights, Jonah needed to acknowledge God's right to spare and love 120,000 pagans. Those ignorant pagans had the right to hear the truth before they were destroyed.

"I Just Want What I Deserve"

I was sitting across my desk from a couple struggling in marriage. The angry partner leaned forward, looked at me, and said, "Pastor, I just want what I deserve out of this relationship, and I am upset because I am not getting it." That's what Jonah was saying.

Have you ever thought or said something like that? "I just want what I deserve. I've got my rights."

I have.

What if you went to God Almighty and said, "God, right this second I want exactly and entirely every single thing I deserve. Because You are a just God I want you to give me exactly what I deserve this moment." It's not a good idea.

I don't think you would like what you'd get. The scriptures tell us that the wages of sin is death (Romans 6:23). Scriptures say that death and hell will be cast into the lake of fire (Revelation 20:14). In one sense, if a just God gave you or me everything we really deserved right now, that would mean immediate death and hell.

Thank God that He treats us with mercy! You know, with that outlook, life is a lot easier. Who cares if I have to go to Nineveh when I should be going to hell? How can I worry about a plant when I should be forever separated from God?

Sinful Anger Ceases When Selfish Rights Are Yielded

How did Jesus avoid being trapped by inappropriate anger? If ever a person had a right to be ticked off by imperfect people, disappointing situations, and violations of rights, it would have been Jesus. Before coming to earth He lived in heaven. He was served by angels. He literally had it all. But note the response of Jesus:

> *Your attitude should be the same as that of Christ Jesus: Who, being in very nature God, did not consider equality with God something to be grasped.*
>
> PHILIPPIANS 2:5–6

Let go of your selfish rights, and you can say good-bye to most of your anger and depression. Let me give you a suggestion that works: When I find self-pity and anger growing inside, I make two lists. First, I jot down everything I'm claiming as a "right." Then, one item at a time, I say, "God, I surrender this to you. I yield this to you. I let go of this right." Then I list everything I have to be thankful for. It is a list of undeserved blessings—more than a hundred at a time, sometimes. And I thank God for every undeserved blessing on the list.

The combination of surrendered rights and active gratitude is powerful. Try it for yourself.

Do You Believe That I Am Able?

MATTHEW 9:28

We all have moments in our lives when we need a miracle. We all face situations that are more than we could possibly handle on our own. We all have needs—financial, spiritual, emotional, physical, familial—that can become overwhelming.

Maybe your issue is not so much a bad thing in your life as it is the absence of something good. You have a dream that is unfulfilled, a desire that is unmet. Maybe it's the need for direction. Sometimes, nothing less than a miracle will do.

Two thousand years ago, two blind men needed a miracle. Matthew tells their story, and in it we will find a dangerous question.

> *As Jesus went on from there, two blind men followed him, calling out, "Have mercy on us, Son of David!"*
>
> *When he had gone indoors, the blind men came to him, and he asked them,* **"Do you believe that I am able to do this?"**
>
> *"Yes, Lord," they replied.*
>
> *Then he touched their eyes and said, "According to your faith will it be done to you"; and their sight was restored.*
>
> MATTHEW 9:27–30

The Need: Two Blind Men Want Sight

In Jesus' time, the blind were societal outcasts. Many people thought they had been judged unworthy by God Himself. Robbed of sight, they lived in a world that robbed them of worth. The Pharisees even taught that people were blind because of sin—either they or their parents, it was assumed, had been wicked.

Probably blind from birth, these two men had never enjoyed the thrill of seeing a sunset or a flower. Jobless and homeless, they usually owned nothing more than discarded junk. They lived on scraps and charity handouts. Their world had always been dark and lonely. Apart from each other, they really had nothing. Life was a fearful battle for survival.

They were desperate.

They couldn't take it any longer.

They needed help.

These blind men went beyond the fact of admitting their need to the point of doing something about it. What did they do? They sought Jesus.

Following Jesus, they cried out for help. Just a year before in their town, Jesus had healed a number of people, including a leper. Undoubtedly, they were thinking, "If He would heal a leper then maybe, just maybe, He'll heal us."

As I picture these two men in my mind, I imagine one as more skeptical and jaded than the other. I can see him shaking his head and mumbling, "What can this Jesus do for us? We're blind, remember? God is punishing us. And you want us to go out in the crowd and make a spectacle of ourselves? I don't know what's gotten into you. Why seek a miracle from a stranger? Don't you know the Pharisees don't like this Jesus?"

But I imagine his friend is different. He responds, "So the Pharisees don't like him? That's one point in His favor! Look,

I think Jesus is someone special. You heard Him yourself the other day near the synagogue. His voice was so clear and powerful—it wasn't the voice of an ordinary man. I believe He can help us. It's worth a try. I'm going to go whether you come or not. I've got to find Jesus."

With that, I see the man getting up to seek out Jesus. His friend doesn't want to be left behind, so he follows. Before long, they approach the center of town and hear the noise of a crowd. It's time to do something desperate.

"Let's call for Him," the first man says. With that, the pair begins to shout out from their darkness, "Jesus, son of David, have mercy on us."

The Question: Do You Believe That I Am Able to Do This?

When he had gone indoors, the blind men came to him, and he asked them, "Do you believe that I am able to do this?"

MATTHEW 9:28

It was a dangerous question for the blind men. If they said no, they doomed themselves to the deepening despair of darkness. If they said yes, they risked additional public embarrassment if Jesus couldn't come through with their miracle. Or, perhaps just as frightening, they faced the threat that He might actually heal them—in which case, they would be responsible for living their lives without any excuses.

So what did they do? How did they answer the question?

Yes, Lord!

They had come too far to turn back.

They had sought out Jesus, crying to him in the crowd. They had followed Him indoors. They had made it this far. This close, they had nothing to lose and everything to gain. So when Jesus asked if the two men believed, a concise answer sprang simultaneously from both sets of lips. They are the words of faith: "Yes, Lord."

They didn't hesitate. They didn't waver. They plunged in. "Yes, Lord."

One thing that distinguishes these blind men from other needy people at that time is the element of *active* faith. What is faith anyway? We could define it as "a conviction that God can and the confident assurance that He will."

These men had a huge, hopeless, overwhelming need, and they wisely added faith to need. Not just "faith in faith," but "faith in Jesus."

Their Sight Was Restored

> *Then he touched their eyes and said, "According to your faith will it be done to you"; and their sight was restored.*
>
> MATTHEW 9:29–30

Faith is one thing God finds irresistible. When He sees it, He's pleased—and He acts.

> *And without faith it is impossible to please God, because anyone who comes to him must believe that he exists and that he rewards those who earnestly seek him.*
>
> HEBREWS 11:6

In this story, we see a pattern that is repeated throughout the Gospels. You could call it a formula for miracles:

NEED + FAITH + JESUS = MIRACLES

Jesus is the key to any miracle. He is the third part of this equation, the most important part. Faith alone does not get the job done. The faith must have the right subject. His name is Jesus.

When you read the Gospels, you see extremely needy people taking a variety of approaches to get to Jesus. A desperate father walked deliberately up to Jesus (Matthew 9:18–19, 23–26). A suffering woman sneaked up behind Him (Matthew 9:20–22). A leper knelt at His feet (Matthew 8:1–3). As we've seen in this chapter, two men literally chased blindly after the Lord. Each one made it to Jesus. Each one had faith. Each one received a miracle.

Let me be perfectly clear: It doesn't matter *how* you come to Jesus, it matters *that* you come to Jesus.

You can take a plane, a bus, or a bicycle. Who cares? What matters is that you get to Jesus. He is the only One who can ultimately meet your need.

Do You Believe?

Do you have a need you can't meet alone? Are you facing a problem that is bigger than you? Is it a relationship, a financial issue, a physical situation? Do you need a miracle today?

Do you have the faith to seek out Jesus? Do you have the faith to pray and turn the matter over to Him? Do you have the faith to step out and do what you know He is telling you to do?

Do you believe He is able?

Whom Shall I Send?
And Who Will Go for Us?

ISAIAH 6:8

Many, many years ago, God asked a young man the same dangerous question He's still asking today.

In 739 BC, Isaiah was brokenhearted, burdened for the state of his nation. Israel had developed commercially and militarily, yet she was rotting spiritually. She was cancerously corrupt and riddled with the putrefying sores of sexual immorality, idolatry, and religion without relationship.

Isaiah loved God passionately and longed to make a difference. Since God knows our hearts, He gave this young man his greatest desire—a glimpse of heaven.

I Saw the Lord

In the year that King Uzziah died, I saw the Lord seated on a throne, high and exalted, and the train of his robe filled the temple.

ISAIAH 6:1

Stop—don't miss those four words: "I saw the Lord." This young man was given a vision only a handful of humans had ever seen. He saw the Lord. He was taken into the throne room of Almighty God.

Isaiah didn't even try to describe God. He is indescribable.

He truly is beyond words. God is infinite, so when we use adjectives like awesome, glorious, majestic, powerful, kind, wise, and compassionate, we are only giving a tiny glimpse of the real thing. We can only guess at what Isaiah saw. In those visionary moments, Isaiah's mind must have exploded with images of the raging fire of holiness, the laser light of purity, the flowing river of wisdom, the roaring ocean of love, the powerful torrent of truth.

The young prophet saw the Lord "seated on a throne." We know from elsewhere in scripture that the throne of God is covered in jewels, radiating rainbows of colors, surrounded in glorious light.

"And the train of his robe filled the temple." Imagine a gigantic, majestic, regal robe of rich red and deep purple so huge that it fills the temple.

> *Above him were seraphs, each with six wings: With two wings they covered their faces, with two they covered their feet, and with two they were flying.*
>
> ISAIAH 6:2

"Above him were seraphs." The beings closest to God are a special type of angel called *seraphim.* That's a Hebrew word meaning "burning ones." Why burning ones? God's holiness is a consuming fire. These seraphim are asbestos angels, burning constantly through eternity in the presence of a holy God.

Holy, Holy, Holy

> *And they were calling to one another: "Holy, holy, holy is the LORD Almighty; the whole earth is full of his glory." At the sound of their voices the doorposts and thresholds shook and the temple was filled with smoke.*
>
> ISAIAH 6:3–4

These glorious angel beings not only burn continuously in the presence of God, they also worship unceasingly in the presence of God. Their praise takes the form of a declaration they can't help but make. The essence of the One before them is so intense that the words flow irresistibly from their lips: "Holy, holy, holy is the LORD Almighty; the whole earth is full of his glory."

Imagine that. Minute after minute, hour after hour, day after day, year after year, decade after decade, century after century, millennium after millennium, these glorious angels sing and shout one word over and over: *Holy, holy, holy.*

Survey American evangelicals to ask what God's primary attribute is and most would probably say, "Love. God is love."

It's true that God is love. But love without holiness is meaningless. The angels closest to God know that the primary attribute of God is *holiness,* a word that means "separation." God is absolutely separate from any and all sin. Through all eternity, the only moment sin and God ever came together was on the cross. Jesus Christ wore our sin as He died for us. It is God's holiness that gives God's love content and strength.

Woe Is Me!

In seeing the Lord, Isaiah was confronted with an astounding awareness of the absolute holiness of God. . .and it terrified him.

> *"Woe to me!" I cried. "I am ruined! For I am a man of unclean lips, and I live among a people of unclean lips, and my eyes have seen the King, the LORD Almighty."*
>
> ISAIAH 6:5

I have often heard people talk about the questions they'd like to ask God when they see Him. Comedians joke about the smart-mouthed things they would say if they were ever in God's presence. But if any of us were to see the Lord today, it would at best be through our fingers—as we cover our faces from His glory, majesty, power, and blazing holiness.

When Isaiah said, "Woe to me," he was acknowledging his sin. He was literally saying, "I am damned, guilty, and condemned to hell." When he said, "I am ruined," he was saying, "I am melting." God is a consuming fire (Hebrews 12:29). When Isaiah saw the undisguised holiness of Almighty God, he knew he deserved eternal punishment in hell. . .and he was crushed.

"Your Guilt Is Taken Away"

> *Then one of the seraphs flew to me with a live coal in his hand, which he had taken with tongs from the altar. With it he touched my mouth and said, "See, this has touched your lips; your guilt is taken away and your sin atoned for."*
>
> Isaiah 6:6–7

Fire can do two things. It can burn and consume, or it can cleanse and purify. The angel took a burning coal from the altar and placed it upon Isaiah's trembling lips. Instead of burning and consuming him, it purified him. What a gracious, merciful, compassionate God we have, one who is willing to cleanse us of our sins!

Isaiah's cleansing occurred more than seven hundred years before the coming of Christ—and provided a temporary relief. When you and I come to God with brokenhearted sorrow and repentance, we are washed with the permanent cleansing of blood, the blood of the Lamb slain for our sins.

"Who Will Go?"

Now that Isaiah was clean before God, he was ready to hear from God. When we are ready to hear, God is ready to speak. Note carefully the dangerous question the Lord asked Isaiah:

> *Then I heard the voice of the Lord saying,* **"Whom shall I send? And who will go for us?"**
>
> ISAIAH 6:8

In 739 BC, God saw what Isaiah saw in His nation, Israel. He saw the sin, the spiritual charades, the cancerous corruption, the religion without relationship. . .and it broke His heart.

The Lord sees the needs of our world today. . .and it still breaks His heart.

He sees the billions of people who do not know Christ and His heart aches. He sees the hungry and homeless and His heart breaks. He sees the villages that have no church. He sees too many Christians wasting their lives on meaningless things and He cries, "Whom shall I send? And who will go for us?"

We must remember that "God so loved *the world*" (John 3:16). The Great Commission is global in scale, as Jesus charged his followers to go "into *all the world*" (Mark 16:15), to "go and make disciples of *all nations*" (Matthew 28:19), and "be my witnesses in Jerusalem, and in all Judea and Samaria, and *to the ends of the earth*" (Acts 1:8). The commission was not to be limited by geography, culture, language, or people. God's heart aches for lost people everywhere, all over the world.

God's Plan

> *"Everyone who calls on the name of the Lord will be saved."*
>
> *How, then, can they call on the one they have not believed in? And how can they believe in the one of whom they have not heard? And how can they hear without someone preaching to them? And how can they preach unless they are sent? As it is written, "How beautiful are the feet of those who bring good news!"*
>
> ROMANS 10:13–15

God's plan for mankind *is* mankind. He does not use angels or special writing in the clouds to spread the gospel. He uses men and women totally committed to Him. He uses young men and women willing to die for Him—and willing to live for Him.

God doesn't see only the world's needs. He's also looking for solutions to those needs. At this very moment, He sees you as a potential answer to the needs of this world. He is asking you a most dangerous question: "Will you go?"

I believe that, just as the angels are perpetually crying out "Holy, holy, holy" because they can't help it, God is constantly crying out, "Who will go?" He can't help it, either.

Here Am I. Send Me!

When you read Isaiah's story, you get a picture of God in His throne room, and you also see His holy angels. As far as we know, the only human present was Isaiah. I find it amusing and insightful that God apparently looked around the room, saw only Isaiah, and yet asked the question,

"Whom shall I send? And who will go for us?"

ISAIAH 6:8

Isaiah must have sensed all the angels looking expectantly at him. I imagine he gulped and raised his hand like an excited first grader saying, "Here am I. Send me!"

Isaiah already had a burden. He already had a passion. He was just waiting for his calling. When it came he responded, "Here am I. Send me."

He was saying, "Lord, here, take all of me. Here is my past, my present, my future. I give you all of me—my dreams, my hopes, my aspirations. Here I am. Send me. I'm available. Use me. Send me to turn Judah back to You. Send me to my people. Send me."

God didn't hesitate.

Go Tell

He said, "Go and tell this people."

ISAIAH 6:9

God's message to Isaiah wasn't particularly happy. But the Lord has a strategy for winning the world back to Himself— and He does that by *sending* men and women who will *go*. It is interesting that the last words of Jesus are:

"As the Father has sent me, I am sending you."

JOHN 20:21

"Go and make disciples of all nations."

MATTHEW 28:19

"Go into all the world and preach the good news to all creation."

MARK 16:15

Want to make a difference in the world? Often, we are the answer to our own prayers. I know of three things that are vitally true of every person reading this book: 1) we need God; 2) we need each other; and 3) *others need us*. Jesus' hands are you and I. The Word of God will only come to the hurting, needy people of this world through our mouths.

When God called me to be saved, I was sitting in a church. When God called me to full-time ministry, I was sitting in a bathtub. When God called me to plant a church, I was sitting on church steps reading a book. When God calls some of you, it may be as you read this book.

Today God is calling His people to ministry. Maybe you are hearing God's call right now. Will you answer His dangerous question by saying, "Yes, Lord. I will go. Here am I, send me"?

What Will Be the Sign of Your Coming?

MATTHEW 24:3

One of my favorite stories concerns a college freshman who was really enjoying his first year away from Mom and Dad. His first semester was so much fun that he hadn't studied at all. Prior to Parents Weekend, he e-mailed his mother:

Having a great time.
Flunking all my classes.
Prepare Pop.

Mom e-mailed back:

Pop prepared.
Prepare yourself!

Like our careless scholar, we also need to be prepared—for the soon return of Jesus Christ. Let me explain.

The Dangerous Question

It had been a whirlwind week. First, Jesus had ridden a donkey into Jerusalem, symbolizing His Messiahship. He had cleansed the temple in an act of righteous indignation. Angry religious leaders had tried to trap and expose Jesus with rhetorical dilemmas. But He had repeatedly tied up His questioners in the cords of their own words.

As Jesus and His disciples left the temple area, the Lord made a stunning prediction. Indicating the grand worship center, He said,

> *"Do you see all these things?" he asked. "I tell you the truth, not one stone here will be left on another; every one will be thrown down."*
>
> MATTHEW 24:2

The disciples' minds probably ran to various Old Testament teachings on the end times. So they asked Jesus a dangerous question:

> *As Jesus was sitting on the Mount of Olives, the disciples came to him privately. "Tell us," they said, "when will this happen, and **what will be the sign of your coming** and of the end of the age?"*
>
> MATTHEW 24:3

What Will Be the Sign of Your Coming?

Are we seeing signs of the end times? Is the end really near? How close are we to the Tribulation and Armageddon? How can we know?

These are dangerous questions. How we answer them affects how we live our lives today.

Recently, for six weeks, I took the challenge of reading the front section of a large daily newspaper through the lens of Bible prophecy. I was stunned. Every day I found at least one article that had a potential bearing on the last days.

Just as highway signs provide information, give direction,

and offer warning, prophetic signs prepare us for the future. Many of them involve the seven years of the Tribulation period. We are told what reality will be *then*. Our challenge is to see what's happening *now* and decide if that indeed is a birth pang of the end. If so, those events and conditions can be considered "signs of the times."

The disciples asked, "What will be the sign of your coming and of the end of the age?" In doing so, they gave Jesus the opportunity to describe several signs of the times. In the rest of this chapter, let's look at some of the major indicators that we are living in the last days.

Major Signs of the End Times

1. *Increasing Natural Disasters.* Jesus answered His disciples' question by describing some of what will happen during the Tribulation as it relates to Israel:

> *"Watch out that no one deceives you. For many will come in my name, claiming, 'I am the Christ,' and will deceive many. You will hear of wars and rumors of wars, but see to it that you are not alarmed. Such things must happen, but the end is still to come. Nation will rise against nation, and kingdom against kingdom. There will be famines and earthquakes in various places. All these are the beginning of birth pains."*
>
> MATTHEW 24:4–8

Note the phrases "famines and earthquakes" and "the beginning of birth pains." One major sign of the end times will be an increase in natural disasters. Jesus mentioned two specifically, saying they will be the "beginning" of birth pains. Birth pains begin weakly and infrequently; an increase in occurrence and intensity leads up to the big event—the birth of a baby. Similarly, a steady increase in natural disasters points to a big (the biggest) event—the second coming of Christ and the time of the end.

What other disasters might herald the end times? The book of Revelation indicates that the third horseman of the apocalypse carries famine (Revelation 6:5–6). Today, we are seeing some of the worst famines in history. In the early 1980s, millions of Africans died of starvation caused by what some news sources called a "famine of biblical proportions." Today, two decades later, twice as many are dying of starvation.[1]

In recent years we've seen record numbers killed by tornadoes, typhoons, and other severe storms. Think of the giant tsunami that killed nearly two hundred thousand people in Indonesia or Hurricane Katrina, which was one of the deadliest storms in United States history.

2. *Moral Disintegration.* Note carefully what the apostle Paul wrote to Timothy, nineteen hundred years ago:

> *But mark this: There will be terrible times in the last days. People will be lovers of themselves, lovers of money, boastful, proud, abusive, disobedient to their parents, ungrateful, unholy, without love, unforgiving, slanderous, without self-control, brutal, not lovers of the good, treacherous, rash, conceited, lovers of pleasure rather than lovers of God—having a form of godliness but denying its power. Have nothing to do with them.*
>
> 2 TIMOTHY 3:1–5

The Bible predicts that, in the last days, moral disintegration will create perilous times. Pockets of moral meltdown have always occurred in societies, but many see a larger, more widespread problem on the rise. Bible scholar

Tim LaHaye, speaking on the end times, has said, "List the eighteen conditions the prophet foretells for the last days. Then examine your daily newspaper, and you will agree: They are already here."[2]

3. *Geo-Political Positioning.* Certain geographic and political events are indicators of the end times. First is the rebirth of Israel, the most amazing nation on earth. With a population less than that of Los Angeles and a landmass less than that of Massachusetts, Israel annually receives the third most media attention of all the nations of the world. Little wonder, since it has the highest per capita number of news correspondents in the world.[3]

The Bible predicted Israel would be scattered and the Holy Land under Gentile control until the last days, when Israel would be regathered to her homeland (Luke 21:24; Ezekiel 38:8, 39:27–28; Jeremiah 23:7–8). Astoundingly, in 1948, Israel became a nation—and since 1948, Jews have been migrating to Israel from all over the world.

Twenty-five hundred years ago, the prophet Daniel wrote that, at the beginning of the Tribulation, the antichrist would sign a peace treaty with Israel (Daniel 9:27). In order for this to occur, Israel had to be a nation and war had to be a threat. Israel has been a nation for some sixty years, and is under a continual threat from her Islamic neighbors, who have a stated goal of wiping the Jewish nation off the face of the earth. They tried in 1967 and in 1973, but both times God miraculously intervened to preserve the grossly outmanned Jews against Arab aggression.

Due to the growing power of her enemies and concessions forced on her regarding the Palestinians, Israel has become a battle zone of suicide bombers, rocket attacks, and other means of violence. Israelis awaken each morning with the possibility of all-out war. Many long for a peace treaty.

Meanwhile, the Bible indicates that in the last days, Europe will be united in a multinational confederacy under the ultimate leadership of the antichrist. He will use this platform to pursue the establishment of a one-world government, a one-world economy, and a one-world military (Daniel 7; Revelation 13).

Twenty years ago, such unity was considered impossible— because European nations had such a history of fighting amongst themselves. Yet, in 1989, the Berlin Wall came down, and in 1993 the seemingly impossible happened: Nations of the European Common Market agreed to create a single economic market. United Europe now rivals the United States, with 345 million people from twelve nations engaging in unrestricted trade with a common currency. That currency, the Euro, gives Europe complete economic unity for the first time in seventeen hundred years—since the Romans ruled the world. The Western European Union is already positioned to be the single European military machine.[4]

4. *Technological Advances and an Information Explosion.*
Writing two thousand to twenty-five hundred years ago, biblical prophets were limited to the language and understanding of their times. Gunpowder, airplanes, television, satellites, computers, helicopters, tanks, missiles, space travel, and nuclear bombs had yet to be invented. But today, for the first time in human history, the technology needed to fulfill the Bible's prophetic predictions is well in place. For example, the Bible speaks of:

a) *Huge numbers killed in the battles of Armageddon* (Revelation 9:13–19,14:17–20, 16:12–16, 19:17–18; Ezekiel 39:1–9). Since 1945, with the invention of the nuclear bomb, this has been entirely possible.

b) *A universal identifying "mark of the beast" on people's hands or heads by which cashless banking is transacted* (Revelation 13:15–18). This seemed bizarre until recently. But the technology is now in place for a single card that contains all the information and identification a person could ever need: medical history, credit card and banking information, photo identification, etc.

Biochips, the size of a piece of uncooked rice, have been created to track lost pets, and, more recently, lost children. These devices can bounce a signal off a satellite onto a police department computer screen, helping officers find a missing child. Laws have been proposed to install such chips in soldiers to carry their medical and financial information and in criminals and terrorists to allow authorities to track them anywhere in the world. Do you see where this is heading?

With such technology, it is now possible for a world dictator to impose complete tyranny. There would be no way to fight back. The birth pains of the rise of antichrist are happening before our very eyes.

c) *The whole world seeing the dead bodies of God's witnesses in Jerusalem* (Revelation 11:7–10). Until recent years, this was not possible. But satellite technology now allows us to see what is happening around the world live, as it occurs, without leaving our own living rooms.

d) *An information explosion* (Daniel 12:4). "Many will go here and there to increase knowledge," Daniel predicted. Through computers and the Internet, each of us now has access to more information than we could possibly ever use.

Are You Ready?

I believe the prophetic end-times clock, after almost two thousand years of silence, began ticking in 1948. It's been ticking louder and faster ever since. The birth pains are coming closer and closer together. The scene is set.

How near are we to the end? No one knows for sure. But we definitely need to be ready.

Notes

1. "Ethiopia: More Aid, More Hunger Still," BBC News, Famine in Africa, http://news.bbc.co.uk/1/hi/in_depth/africa/2002/famine_in_africa/default.stm (accessed June 25, 2007).
2. Tim LaHaye, October 2, 2005, at Thomas Road Baptist Church's annual Super Conference.
3. Ed Hindson, *Final Signs* (Eugene, OR: Harvest House, 1996), pp. 105, 106.
4. Ibid.

Who Is It You Are Looking For?

JOHN 20:15

A man once told me that for him to become a genuine follower of Jesus Christ, he would need to leave his brain at the door. Christianity, he said, is an irrational, anti-intellectual, sentimental, and purely emotional leap in the dark.

I strongly disagree. Some of the greatest minds in history have been devoted followers of Jesus Christ. Christianity is the only belief system that is both logically sensible and spiritually powerful.

It is not intellectual suicide to place faith in Jesus Christ. He died to take away our sins, not our brains.

Some have defined faith as "believing in spite of the facts." I have found true faith to be "believing *because* of the facts." And I'm not the only one. Some of the first to believe *because* of the facts were Peter, John, and Mary Magdalene.

"Who Is It You Are Looking For?"

Early on the first day of the week, while it was still dark, Mary Magdalene went to the tomb and saw that the stone had been removed from the entrance. So she came running to Simon Peter and the other disciple, the one Jesus loved, and said, "They have taken the Lord out of the tomb, and we don't know where they have put him!"

So Peter and the other disciple started for the tomb. Both were running, but the other disciple outran Peter and reached the tomb first. He bent over and looked in at the strips of linen lying there but did not go in. Then Simon Peter, who was behind him, arrived and went into the tomb. He saw the strips of linen lying there, as well as the burial cloth that had been around Jesus' head. The cloth was folded up by itself, separate from the linen. Finally the other disciple, who had reached the tomb first, also went inside. He saw and believed.

JOHN 20:1–8

Seeing the empty tomb, and especially the unique way the grave clothes were laid, was enough for John ("the other disciple, the one Jesus loved"). Peter was still processing the scene (Luke 24:12). Mary also needed some convincing.

Mary stood outside the tomb crying. As she wept, she bent over to look into the tomb and saw two angels in white, seated where Jesus' body had been, one at the head and the other at the foot.

They asked her, "Woman, why are you crying?"

"They have taken my Lord away," she said, "and I don't know where they have put him." At this, she turned around and saw Jesus standing there, but she did not realize that it was Jesus.

"Woman," he said, "why are you crying? **Who is it you are looking for?***"*

JOHN 20:11–15

Mary was stunned by the disappearance of Jesus' body from its tomb. Even the sight of angels failed to convince her of the Lord's resurrection. But then Jesus Himself stood before her and, I believe, playfully asked her a dangerous question:

"Who is it you are looking for?"

> *Thinking he was the gardener, she said, "Sir, if you have carried him away, tell me where you have put him, and I will get him."*
>
> *Jesus said to her, "Mary."*
>
> *She turned toward him and cried out in Aramaic, "Rabboni!" (which means Teacher).*
>
> *Jesus said, "Do not hold on to me, for I have not yet returned to the Father. Go instead to my brothers and tell them, 'I am returning to my Father and your Father, to my God and your God.' "*
>
> *Mary Magdalene went to the disciples with the news: "I have seen the Lord!" And she told them that he had said these things to her.*
>
> JOHN 20:15–18

Those who sincerely look for Jesus will find Him. Many are the skeptics who've come to faith when confronted with the facts of Jesus' resurrection. No one has ever successfully denied or disproved the empty tomb. They've tried, but their explanations don't stand up to the primary proofs of the resurrection.

The Testimony of the Empty Tomb

One of the primary proofs of the resurrection is that shortly after Jesus was crucified and buried, His tomb was found to be vacant. There was no body. How could that be?

1) *Did He Swoon?* Some skeptics say Jesus didn't really rise from the dead, because He never died in the first place. He merely "swooned" on the cross and revived in the cool of the tomb.

But the facts make this theory impossible to believe. Jesus was definitely dead on the cross. He had been scourged prior to the crucifixion (Matthew 27:26–28). Historically, a scourging stopped at thirty-nine lashes, as forty were considered fatal. So Jesus was more than half dead even before being placed on the cross.

Shortly before the crucifixion, Jesus had sweat blood (Luke 22:44), had a crown of thorns smashed on his head (Matthew 27:27–29), and was beaten on the head with a stick (Matthew 27:30).

On the cross, Jesus uttered a death cry: "It is finished" (John 19:30). When a Roman soldier stuck a spear in Jesus' side, blood and water flowed out (John 19:34). Blood and water do not separate unless a person is dead.

The Romans were convinced Jesus was dead. Crucifixion is a hideously slow and painful style of execution, as victims expired from lack of air. Spiked to the cross, they fought for every breath, pushing and pulling, working their way up and down for oxygen. When they no longer had strength or will to push against the spikes, they would suffocate. With the Jewish Sabbath beginning Friday at sunset, the Romans would hasten the criminals' deaths and remove them from their crosses. Soldiers broke the legs of the two thieves (John 19:31–32) so they could no longer push up and therefore no longer breathe. But when they came to Jesus, the soldiers didn't need to break his legs (John 19:33–34). Why? The answer is evident—Jesus was already dead.

After Jesus was taken off the cross, His body was wrapped in linen soaked with spices (John 19:38–40). The aromatic scents were poured into each layer of the linen grave wrappings and could weigh up to a hundred pounds. Jesus' friends wouldn't have done this if He wasn't already dead.

Finally, here's a good question: "How could a man who had been beaten nearly to death, who had been hanging on a cross for six hours, and who had been wrapped in very heavy grave clothes get up by himself, work his way out of his wrappings, move the large stone from the grave entrance, and overpower the guards stationed there?" The answer is simple: He could not. The evidence is clear—Jesus did not swoon. He was dead.

Only the resurrection explains the empty tomb.

2) *Did the Disciples Go to the Wrong Tomb?* Some try to explain the empty tomb by another theory: On Sunday morning, the women and the disciples went to another tomb that just happened to be empty. But this theory has holes, too. Remember, those women were there when Jesus was placed in the tomb (Luke 23:55)—they knew which tomb it was. Plus, the tomb had a Roman seal and a Roman guard (Matthew 27:62–66). No other tomb would have that.

But suppose the women and the disciples somehow did go to the wrong tomb. Why would the Jewish leaders and Roman soldiers then invent a story that the body had been stolen (Matthew 28:11–15)? In order to silence the disciples, Jesus' enemies could simply lead all the disciples to the right tomb, open it, and show them the dead body of Jesus Christ.

3) *Was the Body Stolen?* Some doubters argue that Jesus' body was stolen either by His disciples (to create an appearance of resurrection) or by His enemies (so his disciples couldn't steal the body).

But the facts tell us the disciples did nothing of the sort. They didn't even believe the resurrection themselves, as they were scared and hiding (John 20:19). Roman soldiers, the most professional, best trained on earth, were there to keep anyone from stealing anything. There is no way a group of common men and women could have taken the body.

Beyond that, the disciples would not steal Jesus' body only

to face certain persecution and death for a known lie. Most of the disciples died ugly martyrs' deaths for preaching the resurrection of Jesus Christ. Let me ask you: Would you die for a lie? Would you die for a lie you *knew* was a lie? Of course not—and neither did they.

As for the idea of Jesus' enemies stealing the body, it makes no sense. First, they had no motive. Second, if they had His body, why not simply produce it to silence the disciples who began to preach Jesus' resurrection? They produced no body *because* they had no body. They had no body *because* Jesus rose from the dead.

The Testimony of Eyewitnesses

Many people saw Jesus after He rose from the dead. One legitimate eyewitness can turn a legal trial upside down—but the eyewitness testimony regarding Jesus' resurrection dwarfs that. Jesus was seen on more than a dozen occasions by more than five hundred people. He was seen in the city and in the country, inside and outside, during the day and at night. He was seen by a variety of people. Some of them had been his followers prior to his resurrection, but others had not.

More impressive is the way the lives of those eyewitnesses changed as a result of what they saw. The disciples went from cowards to crusaders, from hiding in fear to preaching in public. Peter, Andrew, Philip, Simon the zealous, James the son of Alphaeus, and Bartholomew were all later crucified. Peter was crucified upside down. Matthew and James, the brother of John, were beheaded. Thaddeus was shot to death by archers.

Even more compelling is the change in those who had doubted. Two of the most amazing eyewitnesses were Jesus' half brothers, Jude and James. Neither believed that Jesus was the Christ prior to His resurrection (John 7:5). In fact, they thought he was crazy (Mark 3:21). But after they saw Jesus crucified and resurrected, they became believers and leaders in the church. Both wrote letters in our New Testament bearing their names. James was later stoned to death for preaching the resurrection of Jesus. Let me ask you again: Do you really think these men would die for a lie?

Thomas, the doubter, met the resurrected Jesus and fell to his knees crying, "My Lord and my God (John 20:28). Paul, the Christian-killer, got on his face and called Jesus "Lord" (Acts 9:5). Paul spent the rest of his life spreading the word of the living Lord Jesus to the world and ended up beheaded for his belief in the resurrected Jesus Christ.

He's Alive!

Christianity is no dead religion. It's not a set of legalistic rules, dull routines, or lifeless rituals. It is a vital relationship with a living, loving God.

Jesus is alive. The empty tomb proves it. The eyewitnesses and their changed lives verify it.

Jesus is alive. He still changes lives today. He still empowers disciples to change the world. He still heals broken hearts.

Who is it you are looking for? Jesus is everything you need.

Who Shall Separate Us from the Love of Christ?

ROMANS 8:35

Does God really love you?

Have your circumstances ever pressed you to doubt His love? Have you ever heard a voice in your head whispering notions such as:

> *God must not really love you.*
> *If God really loved you, He would not have let this happen to you.*
> *God may love you, but not as much as He loves other people.*
> *You don't deserve God's love.*
> *Why should God love someone like you?*

If ever a man had reason to question God's love, it would be the apostle Paul. He devoted his life to serving Christ, yet most of what he got in return was deep frustration and violent adversity. Draining work, difficult travel, sleepless nights, raw injustice, and ugly betrayal filled his résumé. Frequent trips to jail, plentiful beatings, even visits to death's door were part of his portfolio. Paul's sorrows were so numerous he had reason to wonder if he was truly the undisputed champion of pain (see 2 Corinthians 11:23–27). Such severe sufferings prompted Paul to ask a series of questions, culminating in the most dangerous of all:

What, then, shall we say in response to this?
If God is for us, who can be against us?
He who did not spare his own Son, but gave him
up for us all—how will he not also, along with him,
graciously give us all things?
Who will bring any charge against those whom God
has chosen? . . .
Who is he that condemns? . . .
Who shall separate us from the love of Christ?
ROMANS 8:31–35

Nothing Shall Separate Us from the Love of Christ

What would make you doubt God's love? Relentless troubles or hurtful hard times? Facing hatred, hunger, or homelessness? What about painful persecution, betrayal by friends or family, or, worse yet, your own awful sins? What is so severe as to strangle the flow of God's love into your life? In other words, "What can separate you from God's love?"

The answer is *nothing*! There is not one thing evil enough, ugly enough, heinous enough, deep enough, or powerful enough to stop God from loving you. Nothing anyone could possibly do to you can sever that connection. Nothing you could ever do to yourself can dam the unstoppable love of God.

Who can separate you from the love of God? A fierce persecutor? A past abuser? Does a supernatural power—an angel, devil, or demon—have that power? Can you separate yourself from the love of God? No. Absolutely nothing can separate you from God's love!

They kill us in cold blood because they hate you.
We're sitting ducks; they pick us off one by one. None

*of this fazes us because Jesus loves us. I'm absolutely
convinced that nothing—nothing living or dead, angelic
or demonic, today or tomorrow, high or low, thinkable or
unthinkable—absolutely nothing can get between us and
God's love because of the way that Jesus our Master has
embraced us.*

ROMANS 8:37–39 THE MESSAGE

In other words, there "ain't nothin' or nobody" big enough,
bad enough, dark enough, or strong enough to keep God from
loving you. His love for you is unimaginable, unconditional,
undeniable, and immeasurable. It is unrelenting, unceasing,
and unstoppable.

Love Greater Than Horrible Loss

On September 11, 2001, Lisa Beamer's husband, Todd, was
killed opposing terrorists on United Airlines Flight 93. Days
after the loss, she stood firm in the love of God.

*God knew the terrible choices the terrorists would make
and that Todd Beamer would die as a result. He knew
my children would be left without a father and me
without a husband. . . . Yet in His sovereignty and in His
perspective on the big picture, He knew it was better to
allow the events to unfold as they did rather than redirect
Todd's plans to avoid death. . . . I can't see all the reasons
He might have allowed this when I know He could have
stopped it. . . . I don't like how His plan looks from my
perspective right now, but knowing that He loves me
and can see the world from start to finish helps me say,
"It's OK."*[1]

Love Greater Than Sin

You know the story: King David made the mistake of growing complacent in his spiritual and professional life. When he should have been leading his troops into battle, he was back at home, restless and bored. When temptation came in the form of the shapely Bathsheba, he did not resist. Before he awoke from his spiritual stupor, he had committed adultery—and murder. The bodies of a betrayed soldier and a wrongly conceived baby were left in the wake of the king's quest for pleasure. It took the piercing rebuke of the prophet Nathan to bring David back to his senses.

Then David found the awful weight of his guilt to be a crushing reality. In extreme contrition, he finally owned up to his sin and went to God who, instead of handing down burning judgment, offered the cool, refreshing waters of mercy and forgiveness. David discovered that nothing—not even his own heinous sin—could separate him from God's love.

Several psalms record David's journey to cleansing and the amazing power of God's love. Here are parts of two:

Generous in love—God, give grace! Huge in mercy—wipe out my bad record. Scrub away my guilt, soak out my sins in your laundry. I know how bad I've been; my sins are staring me down.

PSALM 51:1–3 THE MESSAGE

Count yourself lucky, how happy you must be—you get a fresh start, your slate's wiped clean. Count yourself lucky— GOD holds nothing against you and you're holding nothing back from him.

When I kept it all inside, my bones turned to powder, my words became daylong groans. The pressure never let up; all the juices of my life dried up. Then I let it all out;

I said, "I'll make a clean breast of my failures to GOD."
Suddenly the pressure was gone—my guilt dissolved,
my sin disappeared.

PSALM 32:1–5 THE MESSAGE

God's love is so vast it surpasses our greatest sins.

Love, No Matter What

To show the Pharisees that God values all people, including
the worst of sinners, Jesus told stories of a lost coin, a lost
sheep, and a lost son (Luke 15).

The lost boy is well known as the "prodigal son." In
the epitome of disrespectfulness, this young man asked for
his inheritance while his father was still living. To make
matters worse, he left home and promptly squandered the
money in wild living. When his cash disappeared, so did
his friends—and he was reduced to feeding pigs to make a
meager living.

When his hunger and humiliation became too much, the
young man came to his senses, deciding he would return home
and beg for the chance to eat at his father's table as a hired
man. But the boy underestimated the power of his father's
love. No amount of personal pain and public shame was great
enough to separate the prodigal son from the love of his father.
As the boy shuffled home, broken and empty, his waiting
father saw him coming.

"But while he was still a long way off, his father saw him
and was filled with compassion for him; he ran to his son,
threw his arms around him and kissed him."

LUKE 15:20

Amazing! The father had every right to disown the boy—
but this father had no such intention. We might expect him,
at best, to let the boy eat with the servants—but this father
went far beyond that. We could imagine the father perhaps
biting his tongue and greeting the boy with folded arms and a
disappointed sneer—but not this father. He *ran* to his son. He
threw his arms around him and kissed him. That is inseparable
love.

But the father didn't even stop there. When the son tried
to grovel, the man would have none of it.

> *"The father said to his servants, 'Quick! Bring the best
> robe and put it on him. Put a ring on his finger and
> sandals on his feet. Bring the fattened calf and kill it. Let's
> have a feast and celebrate. For this son of mine was dead
> and is alive again; he was lost and is found.' So they began
> to celebrate."*
>
> LUKE 15:22–24

The father in the story, of course, is God Himself. His love
is so immense it overwhelms our selfish rebellion.

More Love Than You Can Imagine

More than a thousand years ago, a Jewish poet penned a
stunning poem, a stanza of which was later found scrawled on
the cold stone wall of an insane asylum. That poem, converted
into a Christian hymn by Frederick M. Lehman in 1917, bears
dramatic testimony to the fact that nothing can separate us
from the love of God.

> *Could we with ink the ocean fill,*
> *And were the skies of parchment made,*

Were every stalk on earth a quill,
And every man a scribe by trade,
To write the love of God above,
Would drain the ocean dry.
Nor could the scroll contain the whole,
Though stretched from sky to sky.[2]

Nothing can separate us from the love of God. Not the stone walls of an asylum. Not even the challenges of mental illness.

I have no idea what threatens your sense of God's love. I can't say what is attempting to come between you and God. But I know one thing for sure: There is nothing that can separate you from the love of God.

Notes

1. Lisa Beamer, quoted in Ann Henderson Hart, "Finding Hope Beyond the Ruins: An Interview with Lisa Beamer," *Modern Reformation*, Vol. 11, No. 5, September/October 2002, pp. 24–25.
2. "History of the Song, '*The Love of God*,'" 200 Amazing Hymn Stories, http://www.tanbible.com/tol_sng/theloveofgod.htm (accessed June 26, 2007).

21

Who Is Worthy?

REVELATION 5:2

Let me tell you a story about an aged pastor named John.
In his younger days, John's spiritual zeal was easily recognized,
and he was given a leadership role in his church. Eventually,
he became an influential pastor and writer.

Late in his life, John's nation went through political
turmoil and spiritual unrest. He was persecuted for his faith.
Pulled away from his home and church, John faced his twilight
years mostly alone and forgotten.

But God never forgets His servants.

One Sunday, as John was having his special time with
the Lord, everything changed. The old man was stunned by
the presence of an angel, one that took John on an amazing
journey. John stepped out of the ordinary and into the
extraordinary—leaving earth for the wonders of heaven, the
"here and now" for the yet-to-come. What he saw and heard
was beyond the experience of any other mortal.

Before him was a stunning throne, encircled by the most
amazing array of color any human had ever seen. Lightning
flashed and thunder roared from the throne, shaking the old
man's bones.

Anchoring the four corners of the throne were giant
angelic beings. Each was a glorious symphony of the familiar—
a lion, an ox, an eagle, a man—and the unfamiliar—with six
wings and eyes all around. They sang in beautiful antiphonal
praise, "Holy, holy, holy is the Lord God Almighty, who was,
and is, and is to come" (Revelation 4:8).

John noticed others around the throne—elders, church leaders, saints. All were wearing pure white robes. Each wore a golden crown. Each was stretched out on his or her face, overwhelmed by the majestic, magnificent glory of the amazing One who sat on the throne.

Before long, a single voice broke through with the most dangerous question of all.

> *Then I saw in the right hand of him who sat on the throne a scroll with writing on both sides and sealed with seven seals. And I saw a mighty angel proclaiming in a loud voice, "**Who is worthy** to break the seals and open the scroll?"*
>
> REVELATION 5:1–2

Who Is Worthy?

Some of the most important questions we can ask include these: Who deserves my heart, mind, soul, and strength? Who merits my love—and my life? Who is worthy of my worship?

Two thousand years ago, the apostle John experienced those questions firsthand in the throne room of heaven. He heard the angel shout, "Who is worthy to break the seals and open the scroll?" He saw the reaction of the assembled multitude.

As I imagine it, John's eyes searched the faces of the human heroes gathered around God's throne. Some in the countless crowd may have pointed to Abraham, the father of God's chosen people. Others put forward Moses the deliverer, or David the shepherd king, or Elijah the prophet, or Daniel the statesman.

Some suggested Mary, the mother of Jesus. Others James, the first martyr, Peter the apostle, or Paul, the genius church planter and author of much of the New Testament. But each of them shrank back in humility and declared themselves, "Unworthy."

No one on earth is worthy.

"Who is worthy?" the angel will cry.

John might look at his own angel guide. Angels are incredibly strong, brilliantly white, servants of God from ages past. *Are you worthy?* John's eyes ask as they meet the eyes of the angel. *No,* the angel shakes his head. *Unworthy.*

"Who is worthy?" the angel cries.

I can even imagine Satan, in his proud, arrogant, defiant way, attempting to take the scroll. But the pretender prince completely misjudges its incredible weight, which drives him to his knees, then flattens him on his back. The color rushes from Satan's face as he fights for breath.

Casually, the One on the throne reaches down and lifts the scroll off Satan's chest.

"Unworthy," the giant angel whispers into the face of the dark prince.

We know that John is weeping, saddened by the complete unworthiness of all who are above the earth, on the earth, or under the earth (Revelation 5:3–4). The harsh reality is this: *No one is worthy.*

The Lion of the Tribe of Judah

But then I imagine a hand gently touching John's arm.

> *Then one of the elders said to me, "Do not weep! See, the Lion of the tribe of Judah, the Root of David, has triumphed. He is able to open the scroll and its seven seals."*
>
> REVELATION 5:5

Lifting his face from his hands, John scans the horizon, eagerly searching for a glorious king—regal, royal, majestic, and magnificent—a lionlike Lord with a golden crown and giant scepter.

But what John sees next stuns him. At center stage, on the throne, surrounded by the angels and the elders is no powerful lion.

> *Then I saw a Lamb, looking as if it had been slain,*
> *standing in the center of the throne.*
>
> REVELATION 5:6

John notices the Lamb had at one time been wonderfully white, pure, innocent, and holy. But now its coat is covered in blood. Beaten and bruised, a crown of thorns hangs on its head.

The Lamb that John sees, which we will one day see, is *the* Lamb of God who takes away the sin of the world. He is the One wounded for our transgressions, bruised for our iniquities, sacrificed for our sins.

Slowly, joyfully, mightily, triumphantly the Lamb will hoist the weighty scroll over His head. As He does, I envision a transformation: He becomes the true Lion King John had expected.

> *And when he had taken* [the scroll], *the four living*
> *creatures and the twenty-four elders fell down before the*
> *Lamb. Each one had a harp and they were holding golden*
> *bowls full of incense, which are the prayers of the saints.*
> *And they sang a new song:*
> *"You are worthy."*
>
> REVELATION 5:8–9

I believe the crowd will spontaneously drop, as if cut at the knees by a giant sword. Rows of men and women from every age, nation, and tribe will be joined by row after row of bright, strong, proud angels.

A thunderous silence descends on the crowd as each one gasps in a holy hush of acknowledgment. They don't bow—they dive on their faces. They spread out their arms, open their hands, and lay bare their hearts. Tears pour from each eye, sobs piercing the cloud of awful silence.

Then slowly, sweetly, like incense, a song rises from the crowd.

> *"You are worthy to take the scroll and to open its seals, because you were slain, and with your blood you purchased men for God from every tribe and language and people and nation."*
>
> REVELATION 5:9

Though the crowd contains people from every time, place, and language, the swelling song blends as a symphony, a beautiful, harmonic, spontaneous offering of praise.

Because You Were Slain

When the word *slain* is sung, I imagine John recalling himself as a young man—seeing an angry crowd drag Jesus up the hill called Golgotha, helplessly watching the Messiah hang suspended between earth and space. Hanging alone, the sinless Lamb wore the disgusting sins of the whole world—including John's.

> *You are worthy!*
> *You are worthy!*
> *You are worthy because you were slain.*

The song turns from broken to jubilant; mourning is transformed into dancing and sorrow is turned into joy. Every creature in heaven, on earth, and under the earth cries out in unison:

> *"Worthy is the Lamb, who was slain, to receive power and wealth and wisdom and strength and honor and glory and praise! . . . To him who sits on the throne and to the Lamb be praise and honor and glory and power, for ever and ever!"*
>
> REVELATION 5:12–13

Who Is Worthy?

Everything John saw and wrote in the book we call the Revelation points to one dangerous question. It may be the most important question ever asked. It may be the most life- and destiny-defining question ever posed.

It is the question asked by the angel before the throne, the question asked in one form or fashion by every thinking person through the ages. That question is this:

Who is worthy?
Who is worthy of my allegiance?
Who is worthy of my affection?
Who is worthy of my devotion?
Who is worthy of my faith?
Who is worthy of my time, money, and possessions?
Who is worthy of my dreams, hopes, and future?
Who is worthy of my hands, feet, mind, and heart?

Who is worthy?
Who is worthy of my giving?

Who is worthy of my Sunday mornings?
Who is worthy of my purity?
Who is worthy of my living with integrity?
Who is worthy of sharing with friends and strangers?
Who is worthy of my complete trust?

Who is worthy?
Who is worth living for?
Who is worth going to jail for?
Who is worth dying for?

The vote is in. Every precinct has reported.
All the votes are counted. It is unanimous.

"Worthy is the Lamb, who was slain, to receive power and wealth and wisdom and strength and honor and glory and praise!"

REVELATION 5:12

What if you lived every day, for the rest of your life, as the answer to the angel's question?

Conclusion

Every few months, after so many miles, wise car owners take their vehicles to the shop for a checkup. Fluid levels, seals, belts, hoses, tires, and brakes are inspected, in hopes of catching small problems before they become big ones. Neglect in this area can result in costly repairs or even dangerous situations.

In a similar way, people should have a physical checkup each year. Doctors give tests and ask pertinent questions:

"Do you use tobacco?"
"Do you consume alcohol?"
"Have you noticed any changes in your eyesight?"
"Have you had trouble sleeping?"
"How has your energy level been?"

Having a safe and dependable vehicle is important. Our physical health is significant. But far more important is our spiritual state. It affects everything else—and even impacts eternity. So it's essential that we undertake periodic spiritual examinations.

In the previous twenty-one chapters, we have discussed the most dangerous questions in the Bible. These queries could also be described as the most important questions Christ-followers could ask themselves. Read through the following list slowly and thoughtfully, honestly examining yourself in light of each question. Carefully note those for which you are unable to answer yes.

1. Does it amaze you that the God who created the universe is intimately concerned about you? (Psalm 8)

2. Do you believe Jesus is God? (Matthew 16)
3. Do you really love Jesus, more than anything else? (John 21)
4. Is your name known in hell? (Acts 19)
5. Are you loving your neighbors? (Luke 10)
6. Have you allowed the death and resurrection of Jesus to be your bridge to God? (Matthew 27)
7. Have you been born again? (John 3)
8. Do you love God with all of your heart, soul, mind, and strength? (Matthew 22)
9. Would you die for Jesus? (John 13)
10. Do you believe the Bible is the Word of God? (Genesis 3)
11. Do you worship the only true God? (Isaiah 44)
12. Are you living for God's cause? (1 Samuel 17)
13. Are you seizing your God-given opportunities to make a difference for Him? (Esther 4)
14. Will you still serve God even if the blessings go away? (Job 1)
15. Have you moved past a selfish focus on your own personal "rights"? (Jonah 4)
16. Are you trusting God for God-sized things? (Matthew 9)
17. Will you go where God leads? (Isaiah 6)
18. Are you prepared for the return of Jesus Christ? (Matthew 24)
19. Do you know who you're really looking for? (John 20)
20. Are you clinging to God's love no matter what? (Romans 8)
21. Are you living each day as though you truly believe Jesus is worth it? (Revelation 21)

How did you do? Are you a dynamically dangerous disciple of Jesus? Are you a terror to the kingdom of darkness?

How does your response to these questions make you feel:

- Ready to charge hell for Jesus?
- Pleasantly surprised that you did so well?
- Spiritually challenged to make some changes?
- Deeply troubled?

Turn your feelings into prayers. Go to the Lord over your responses. Pursue Him for those areas in which you sense Him wanting you to grow.

Be dangerous for God. It's really the safest way to live.

If you enjoyed

The **21** Most Dangerous
Questions *of the* Bible

look for these other books by
Dave Earley

The 21 Most Effective Prayers of the Bible
ISBN 978-1-59310-605-8
Want to know how to pray? Use the Word of God as
your guide! This easy-to-read volume studies twenty-one
heartfelt prayers from the Bible that produced results.

The 21 Most Encouraging Promises of the Bible
ISBN 978-1-59789-043-4
In need of some encouragement today? God's
Word is packed with wonderful promises—
and here are twenty-one of the best!

The 21 Most Amazing Truths about Heaven
ISBN 978-1-59789-292-6
What is heaven really like? Find out here. Author Dave
Earley delves deeply into scripture to provide *The 21 Most
Amazing Truths about Heaven.*

21 Reasons Bad Things Happen to Good People
ISBN 978-1-59789-661-0
Popular author Dave Earley provides twenty-one
key reasons why God allows bad things
to happen to "good" people.

Available wherever Christian books are sold.